BUCK PETERSON'S

COMPLETE GUIDE TO
DEER HUNTING

BUCK PETERSON'S

COMPLETE GUIDE TO

DEER HUNTING

BY

BUCK "BUCK" PETERSON

ILLUSTRATIONS BY

J. ANGUS "SOURDOUGH" MCLEAN

TEN SPEED PRESS
Berkeley | Toronto

Information contained in this guidebook has been sworn to by
reputable game officials, responsible game biologists, senior park rangers,
and sober old-timers as they could be found. Something could still
go wrong and Buck assumes no responsibility for anything that does.
Ditto Ten Speed Press.

TEN SPEED PRESS
P.O. Box 7123
Berkeley, California 94707

Cover and interior design by Headcase Design
Illustrations by J. Angus "Sourdough" McLean

Distributed in Australia by Simon and Schuster Australia, in Canada by Ten Speed Press
Canada, in New Zealand by Southern Publishers Group, in South Africa by Real Books,
and in the United Kingdom and Europe by Airlift Book Company.

Library of Congress Cataloging-in-Publication Data

Peterson, B. R.
   Buck Peterson's complete guide to deer hunting / by Buck "Buck" Peterson ;
illustrations by J. Angus "Sourdough" McLean.-- Rev.
      p. cm.
   Includes bibliographical references and index.
   ISBN-13: 978-1-58008-738-4 (alk. paper)
   ISBN-10: 1-58008-738-8 (alk. paper)
   1. Deer hunting--Humor. I. Title.
   SK301.P48 2006
   799.2'7652--dc22
                                        2006000187
Printed in the U.S.A.

1 2 3 4 5 6 7 8 9 10 – 10 09 08 07 06

DEDICATION

Deer hunting was introduced and taught to me by two gentlemen of the northern Minnesota woods. It is to these master hunters, my late uncle, George Peterson, and his late hunting buddy, Doc Jarnot, who seasoned my life with hunting health and humor, that this irreverent guide book is re-dedicated.

CONTENTS

INTRODUCTION

Not long ago while Buck was hot on the trail of another record-busting deer in its prime northernmost Minnesota habitat, he was struck by the thought that once he goes to the big hunting camp in the sky, a large gut pile of hunting wisdom may be lost to future generations forever. That certainly would be a fine kettle of camp meats!

First off, let's ask the obvious: "Why, oh why, does Buck hunt deer? Is it for some smarmy reunion with Mother Nature and all her splendors, a soft-focus communion with primal instincts?" Nope. "Is it those troubling dreams of the Great White Whitetail?" Nope.

It's because Buck likes the taste of venison. He likes it fried, broiled, pickled, and jerkied. He likes it for breakfast, brunch, lunch, high tea, early supper, and late-night dinner. If he has a lot, he may share. If he has just a little, it'll be hoarded and the closest you'll get to his pan fry is the smell leaking out under his back door. He likes it raw, red, pink, and burned to a crisp. He likes it on a plate, in his hands, and on the floor. It can be sliced and diced, cubed and coddled, and flaked and baked. He likes to chew it into little pieces and add a few carrots to make a fine "mouth stew." He'll gulp large chunks and force gag reflexes that bring it up for another chew! He'll throw a chop in a Cuisinart for a real Bloody Mary. He'll try to eat it slow but always rushes to the last bite, and lets it die in the back of his mouth to feel the muscle molecules break down in his digestive juices. He'll eat the heart, the liver, the cheeks, the lips, and all but the feathers. Buck is not a happy hunter without venison. And Buck's dreams of the Great White Whitetail are troubling but predictable.

Buck Peterson's Complete Guide to Deer Hunting is for all deer hunters, young and old, tall and short (well, not that short), and men and women, and starts where other deer hunting books leave off. The "Guide" (as it's properly called) is not just another magazine article thinly stretched over the bones of a book. In fact, this is the last book you'll need on deer hunting and it should have been your first. Give all the other books away. There are secrets in the Guide that many famous outdoor writers have tried to learn by following Buck on his trips. Several of the younger, lazier ones have even offered Buck's hunting pals money and excess sporting goods for a few tips and a good map of his hunting grounds. In a rare display of morality, they declined.

The Guide is a working document to follow you everywhere and designed to be put in the glove box of your old F150. It won't guarantee a Boom and Crockpot trophy. It won't even help you shoot a deer. Your odds of seeing one, a good one, especially in Wisconsin, are much too slim for that. It is intended, however, to help you take care of business. This book includes items of protocol, etiquette, and occasionally, endearment; it's, if you will, a Mr. Manners of the woods. It tells you how to be a good guy, a good hunting buddy, a true sportsman, and a major carnivore. It's a little thinner than most guidebooks because Buck doesn't accept any advertising (although he is open to the suggestion) and doesn't include any grainy black and white photos of his camp carnage. However, it is a huge, happy gutpile of suggestions, tips, and anecdotes. If this book doesn't help you blow a hole in a children's book character (you know which one I'm talking about), maybe one of your more successful hunting partners will share some of their children's book character (the one with a name that starts with the letter B and ends in Ambi) with you. It is also a required textbook in Buck Peterson's Wilderness School and Famous Sportsman Correspondence Course and another volume in Buck's paperbound treasury of Guides to Hunting Skills, Manliness, and Outdoor Happiness.

one of two hundred thousand limited edition

THE MOST FREQUENTLY ASKED QUESTIONS ABOUT DEER AND DEER HUNTING

1. **Do deer mate for life, like geese and people who read good books?**

   No. Bucks have the morals of a billy goat, always flirting with the new girls. Does, if they had their druthers (which they don't) would prefer to live a monogamous lifestyle. P.S. Doe druthers are best served al dente.

2. **Do deer really feel like deer, you know, or are they just like people in deer clothing?**

   Only deer that live near people question their "deer-ness." These heightened sensibilities, often found in bucks with one or no testicles, are very dangerous to a deer's survival during hunting season.

3. **Should I hunt early in the season?**

   Yes, deer are more trusting and can even be petted.

4. **Is it okay to shoot that damn fox squirrel making so much noise in that red oak tree?**

   Yes. A headshot is preferred so at least the tail can be salvaged for tying flies.

5. **¿Quién es "Bambi"?**

   Es "camp meat," señor y señorita.

6. **Are the woods just like the books say—fluffy snow, bright colored leaves, crystal-clear reflective ponds, and full of soft cuddly animals with names like Mr. Owl?**

   In Buck's neck of the woods, yes, and his field of fire stands heads and shoulders over other fabled habitat.

7. **How can you tell a buck's age?**

   The antlers start sagging first. Instead of only thinking about romancing the next doe, the older ones concentrate on finding and enjoying a good meal. The real old bucks pray for a painless bowel movement.

8. *My bride-to-be doesn't think game meat is appropriate for the wedding reception.*

   Pregnant women often think that. Congratulations!

9. *What do deer hunting guides do once the non-resident dudes go to bed?*

   Contrary to popular belief, they are not getting gear ready for tomorrow. They are sitting around the campfire, talking and laughing about the bozo non-resident hunters in tents 1 and 2.

10. *Is it okay to use one of those full-size deer decoys game wardens have on your own property?*

    Yes, but if you must smoke inside the decoy, blow the smoke out the anus. Real deer know the dangers of smoking.

11. *Venison makes my wife fart. Big time, nasty ones. She says it's not her and that women don't fart.*

    As a famous comedian once observed, women don't fart but often stand next to a dog that does.

12. *How many shots does it take to kill that big buck on the crossing sign?*

    One shot to the big leg holding him up should tip him over.

13. *Do deer like being deer?*

    Modern stresses and strains are producing increasing numbers of urban deer who would rather be another large animal like a moose or elk. There is no evidence of deer wanting to be a smaller animal like a squirrel.

14. *If you shoot at Bambi and hit Thumper instead, do you need a small game license?*

    No.

15. *How do you hunt bucks during the rut?*

    Shoot the antlered animal on top of the doe.

THE

HUNTED

THE DIFFERENT KINDS

MULE DEER: In Latin, they are called *odocoileus hemionus*, meaning half ass or mule. This is misleading as their hindquarters are very complete and not to be tampered without invitation. It's believed the term refers to the game official who hung the name on them.

Mule deer have thick necks, are easier to hunt than whitetail, and can be fooled by most methods of hunting. They are found in the west, in mountain retreats, but sometimes in open country. Mule deer are built like your mother-in-law—stocky bodies with thick legs and big, ugly feet.

Mulies have large, mule-like ears for listening across mountain passes and a thin tail with a black tip that is left down due to an overriding concern with public decency. Mule deer have the heaviest antlers and are the largest animals in the deer world.

In British Columbia, Canada, mule deer are called a subspecies of black-tailed deer. Once again, those hockey pucks have it all hemionus-backwards.

For those not familiar with Canada, it is the country behind you when you face Mexico.

WHITETAIL DEER: Lewis and Clark, a couple of lost souls from St. Louis, first saw and described this animal as "common deer." They are more properly descendants of "Virginia's deer." The history books are not too clear on who this Virginia was, but it's thought she was a plantation owner's wife who dabbled in animal husbandry without her husband's knowledge. In exchange, she didn't know about his "diddling" in the servants' quarters.

Whitetail deer are found everywhere in North America yet prefer the eastern climates. They are found in abundance lying down, very still, with X's in their eyes near Buck's stand.

The animals are a little smaller, more delicate, and certainly more skittish than their western cousins. They have blacker noses and a white tail and rump. They are slender, dainty, high-strung prima donnas with neuroses only dreamt about by fauna-Freuds. They like to stay close to home, much like their smaller and slower woodland friends. Their tail movements are different than mule deer. When flat or slightly twitching, all is okay. If the tail sticks straight out—danger. If up and waving, that wave is for you.

Subspecies such as Coues deer in New Mexico and Arizona are the preferred target for short people, as these dwarf-like animals with big racks look good hanging in their little houses.

OUT OF SEASON DEER: These animals are a mix of the above, and easier to shoot but more difficult to get home. They are best identified with hand-held spotlights. If a warden comes up to you after you've accidentally shot and started to gut one of these deer, look outraged, pinch the deer's nose shut and start mouth to mouth resuscitation immediately, pushing firmly on the rib cage.

OUT OF RANGE DEER: This animal is a favorite of non-resident hunters and pursued with a volley of shots, swinging wide vertically or horizontally, spraying the bullets in an arc that the critter can't avoid. Fully automatic weapons are used in this shoot. Junior members of the non-resident camp will carry the animal parts out.

CAMP DEER: These animals are the best tasting and are provided by states with an active concern for happy, well-fed hunters who will continue to buy over-priced non-resident licenses. Some states say you have to make all killed game as part of your daily bag. It's not too clear exactly what that means, especially if you are half in the bag once the count begins.

THE DIFFERENT SEXES

MALE: Male deer, or bucks, are the ceremonial head of the deer household and the major breadwinner. They have two key distinguishing features:

✔ *THE ANTLER:* Antlers are racks of calcified bone, and, unlike horns, are shed every year. When this head of "horn" is growing, calcium is pulled from other parts of their body and must be replenished by an extraordinary quantity of acorns, small rodents, truffles, and stuffed wild mushrooms. In the battle for calcium share, the hips usually win, causing the antlers to lose their stiffness and fall loose on the head, flopping like undercooked spaghetti when the buck runs.

P.S. Let's set the record straight. The bone above is not connected to the bone below a buck. Also, for non-resident hunters, the difference between beer nuts and deer nuts is the latter are under a buck.

On rare occasions, game wardens and nature walkabouts have found deer whose calcium had been pulled up so abruptly the leg bones had collapsed, but those deer sure had good-looking racks. The rack is an object of veneration by smaller bucks and by all does. It is the current yardstick to determine trophy animals.

MULE DEER ANTLERS
SINGLE FORKS

WHITETAIL ANTLERS
MULTIPLE FORKS

Antler growth begins with the deer's pineal gland telling the brain to push some velvet-encased blood vessels into the air. A little later, the *cajones* stew up a nice batch of male hormones to tighten them and then stop their growth, cutting off the blood supply. The antlers are now hard and the velvet is rubbed off as it dries. The act of rubbing is an erotic act for trophy hunters.

Occasionally a doe without enough female hormones to block antler growth can sprout male headgear and these unfortunate creatures are called lesbucks by respected game biologists. A change of diet, weekly shots, and herd counseling are only temporary treatments of this difficult, yet, in California more acceptable, condition.

After the hunting season, antlers fall off as the animal walks downhill, leaving big, ugly bald spots. If the bucks in a herd grow their antlers at the same time, they'll shed them at the same time too, setting off such a clatter that does lying in their beds will jump up to see what's the matter. The big bucks will feel extremely lightheaded for a while. A difficult shedding produces severe migraine headaches and is another cross a mature animal must bear.

The size of the antlers is determined by how good the groceries are in the neighborhood, the buck's genes, and the general living conditions of the animal. A very young buck, given the right circumstances, can have a monster rack in the first season, and these child prodigies are very precocious. And very good eating.

✔ *THE SCHWANTZ:* The buck's male organ, or "el grande," once removed from a truly dead animal, is a valuable memento of a good hunt. In many Third World countries and certain neighborhoods in Los Angeles, "los bones" have religious significance and are displayed in shrines with loud, fast, but danceable music. In the loving hands of a craftsman, it can be made into a neat little coin purse and a great gift for the little lady. Remember hunting season is immediately followed by Christmas.

Other distinguishing features include:

✔ *COLOR:* Usually a little darker, especially along the lower cheeks and above the upper lip, producing a shadow late in the day, around 5:00 P.M.

✔ *HAIR DENSITY:* Thick and matted, except in older bucks where hair starts to thin out on top, starting with a small bald spot and spreading in ever-widening circles.

✔ *SPEED:* Similar to does but due to lower appendage must build a bigger head of steam to clear barbed-wire fences.

✔ *HABITS:* Excessive male bonding and promiscuity in early years, maturing to a protective and covetous collection of a large harem.

✔ *HABITAT:* The core areas for a whitetail buck can range from 40 to 50 acres, as they are usually loners. Mule deer bucks are more social and seen hanging around other four-legged large animals, such as moose and elk in the wild, giraffes and hippos in game preserves, and four-wheeled vehicles.

BUCK'S BONUS TIP: Bucks of enormous proportions are today's trophies. They can only be described as the 600-pound gorilla of the deer world. Buck's most recent super-buck is shown below. The Boom and Crockpot measurer quit in amazement.

The best way to tell if you are in a super-buck area is by the gray crotch hair on the upper strands of the barbed wire. If blaze orange threads accompany the hank of gray hair, call 911.

FEMALE: Female deer are called does (sing after me: ♪ doe, a deer, a female deer ♪♪) and are the more passive and submissive sex. In many states, they are reduced to being called "antlerless deer." Under pressure from women's groups, state officials in the blue northeastern states are lobbying to rename "bucks only" seasons to "titless deer only."

Does differ from bucks in their ability to reproduce, and superior social skills. Except for certain times of the month, they seem more even-tempered than the males. As in large Italian families, a mature doe is the real head of the household, regardless of what that lazy bastard downwind says.

Instead of having just two play stations, female deer have a whole flock of nipples along their belly reserved for the feeding of their young. They cannot be used for erotic foreplay. They are just there, much like those of the boss's secretary.

The female organs and the mysterious druthers are where you'd expect them, south of the beltline in a spot called the "Great White North." They are as organized and as complicated as a human's and major playthings in disreputable hunting camps.

The female deer has a reproductive cycle that a buck enjoys pedaling and comes into heat like an eighteen-year-old cheerleader. Increasing irritability marks the gestation period, along with swollen hooves and a higher pitched, whiny bleat. For the most part, deliveries are uneventful, marked only by ungodly screams when male fawns are born with a full rack.

BUCK'S BONUS TIP: **Female deer with large druthers— "superdoes"—are accompanied by several spike bucks and, for reasons not immediately obvious to some, are more likely to be found in states that vote Democrat.**

ENDANGERED SPECIES

Federal and state laws protect animals that can't protect themselves. The two most popular non-shootable meat lockers are:

COLUMBIAN WHITETAIL: Unable to handle the stress of agricultural expansion, these small animals are found only in the Columbia River estuary near Cathlamet, Washington, and Roseburg, Oregon. They are smaller than a German shepherd and much better eating.

KEY DEER: Originally imported to the Florida Keys by well-meaning European drug runners, the dog-sized Key deer were popular pets of large estate owners. Overbreeding pushed their numbers into the wild owned by developers and tour companies were formed to thin out their ranks. More recently, wealthy "snowbirds" and conch store owners in Key West wanted their lively lawn ornaments returned to the old park-like setting and pushed hunting restrictions through a corrupt legislative process. They have initiated a Safe Neighborhood program in the Keys where threatened deer can safely hide in the backyards of homes with the familiar upturned-hand-with-a-deer-hiding-behind-it sign posted on their front lawn. With backstraps the size of a half-dollar, these animals are too small to eat anyway and the meat is tainted by their affection for Key Lime pie.

TROPHY BUCKS IN WISCONSIN: Due to the short supply of qualified resident trophy hunters, Wisconsin game officials are considering the importing of "hired guns" to cull the herds. The sharpshooters would be issued complimentary licenses by means of a direct mail campaign to the membership list of the Disabled and Blind Hunters Association of Minnesota. The overpopulation of trophy animals makes for an anxious wood as the stress of carrying both heavy social burdens and heavy antlers can cause the breakdown of the family unit.

DEER SIGNS

EARLY SIGNS: In caves all over the country, early deer hunters carved their exploits on limestone walls.

    The above sample shows early hunters climbing on their horses to go hunting, proving that backcountry hunters are carrying on traditions of long ago.

MODERN SIGNS AND HOW TO READ THEM: If the deer crossing sign shows running or leaping deer, that's the only kind they have in that area. If the animals are shown standing still, that's what they'll do for you as you take aim. If there are antlers on the deer, it's a buck's only area and if there are lots of deer signs around, that means there are lots of deer around. In Alabama, Arkansas, and parts of Mississippi, these road signs are provided by the state for pre-season target practice.

Some signs just say what they mean!

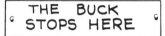

Another deer sign is the presence of tire skid marks and big clumps of hair along the roadside. A fresh gut pile is a dead giveaway. A gut pile as big as the pile of leaves you used to jump in as a kid is a sure sign of super-bucks and Buck himself.

A sure sign of deer:

NATURAL SIGNS: Deer have hoof prints that are easy to follow and look like this:

You can also easily tell the difference between does and bucks. Bucks are heel-heavy and more authoritative. Doe tracks are often wider in the back, due to their child-bearing habits.

A DOE   *A SMALL BUCK*

or a bowlegged young buck from Texas.

Tracks are indications of the activity of the moment. Young deer will drag their feet on the way to a deer event with their folks. Standing deer may have one extra-deep track if they are counting hunters entering the woods and others may only leave two or three tracks if they survived a shotgun season in Michigan.

A REAL BIG BUCK!

More unusual tracks include:

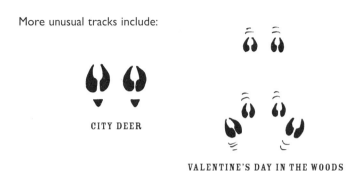

CITY DEER

VALENTINE'S DAY IN THE WOODS

TRACK PATTERNS: You'll find track trails and these highways usually connect all the stops in prime deer habitat: water, food, cover, and protection. You'll want to know where deer drink, eat, sleep, and make little deer.

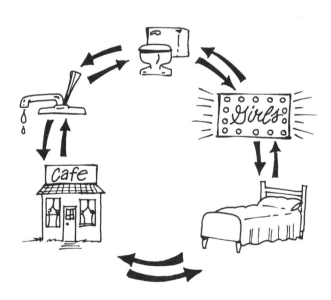

Follow tracks in both directions otherwise you'll get dizzy. Most deer live in a fixed area so if you do this right, you'll never get lost. Well, not really lost. Forty to fifty acres isn't that large an area for search and rescue to cover. Unless it's really cold or snowing. Or your family called off the search.

DROPPINGS: Deer scat is an important sign of animal activity and health. If the poop pellets are in a thin trail spread over a long grunt, the deer was going Big Job on the run and there is no reason to think it'll slow down to wipe.

If the marbles are widely scattered, the deer has been scared scat-less and had an emergency evacuation of the bowels, caused by a true case of Buck (hunter of legend) fever.

If the droppings are stacked in a very neat, precisely arranged pile, you've come upon the embarrassing sign of a girly-man deer.

If the droppings are large, black, and tarry, with pieces of Fritos, Beer Nuts, and an occasional beer bottle cap, your neighbor is in the area.

If you see no scat and know the area has large deer, trophy bucks are holding their poop until they reach deep cover.

Bear and deer scat look a lot alike. It's helpful to know the difference. Bear scat usually tastes highly peppered and may contain a tiny warning bell. Deer scat tastes a lot like your mother-in-law's meatloaf.

Some say they can tell the difference between buck and doe scat. A great white Wisconsin hunter and Buck's good buddy weighs in with this taste test: "Owing to their difference and preferred bedding and eating habits, buck and doe poop do have distinctly different tastes. Bucks, being very secretive and tending to hole up in the most impenetrable woods and swamps, have a decidedly harder taste in their scat. Heavy oak, birch, pine, cattails, and thistle prevail, and therefore buck poop elicits a harder finish. This changes in states like Wisconsin where hunters feed corn to deer. Then corn prevails with the other flavors relegated to the background, but still evident on the palate. On the other hand, does prefer to graze in suburban yards, and exhibit a prevailing aroma of gardenia, tulip, and hosta, with a hint of rose petal. The actual amalgam is a mix of softer and sweeter tastes with a superior bouquet."

DEER SCENTS: Much like you, deer have places on their bodies that don't smell so good.

For example, they have glands between their toes called interdigitals that produce a sticky, yellow toe-jam that stinks like your little brother's. These glands are present on all remaining feet after the shotgun season. When the deer is walking around aimlessly like most animals, some of this gee-gaw goes in the track for another deer to follow. Does can find frisky fawns, and bucks their dreamboats by following this yellow-thick road.

Deer have their armpits down the outside of their hind legs. There are two glands on each leg, one called the metatarsal, located low on the outside and bordered by soft hair. Not much is known about these except that fright triggers excretions. The more active tarsals are found inside each hind leg and surrounded by tufted long hairs. The hairs stand like hackles when the animal is scared or mad. Deer will urinate on these little powder puffs and once mixed with the glands' musk, the combined odor is used by bucks to moisten a scrape in the dirt, and as an all-occasion cologne. When

an animal is spooked, these tarsals will shoot out a stink that'll empty a wood.

The other important gland is the pre-orbital—a small, little-understood gland in the eye that secretes another signature odor and is passed on leaves during a rub. Maybe it's only sleep gunk the animals would rub off if they could get their paws that high. When deer are not crying over their fate as a doomed forest animal, this is the gland that keeps their eyes moist.

SCRAPES: During the rut, bucks leave personalized notes throughout the woods, scraping small areas clear of twigs and leaves, and leaving his scent for a doe in heat to enjoy.

Scrapes let the does know where the big guy will be. These little pee Post-Its are oval dirt depressions six to twenty inches across, and in an area where the buck feels most manly. Active breeding scrapes are seven feet in diameter and drive the ladies crazy.

If you see several scrapes within a single area in good cover, you are in a Bambi brothel and should stand close enough to catch all the illicit action. Attracted by a good scrape, does will come by, take a number, and sit in the big buck's waiting room.

Doe scrapes are increasing in number. Like most Lutheran women, does are embarrassed by their bottoms and by what happens down there. The prudish does cover their droppings by kick-scraping a dirt cover.

Bucks scrape a line around their core area. Since whitetails live in a square mile or so, it takes a full summer of scraping to make the circle, especially with pesky young bucks messing up the lines. Mule deer find this task almost impossible.

THE RUB: Bucks like to rub trees and branches with their headgear for three reasons:

✔ To establish a territory.
✔ To rub old velvet from the new antlers.
✔ To rearrange head lice.

Does enjoy a quick rub on the D spot, an erogenous zone right below the tail. Fawns rub short bushes to get rid of their spots.

If you see rubs, most likely a buck is in the neighborhood. Good rubs are bright and shiny from regular use. Dull rubs are from dull deer you don't want to shoot anyway.

During preseason, check for rubs in conjunction with beds and droppings. Several rubs in a row are called a rub line. If you tie a string between each, you'll earn a merit badge and face true north, as opposed to magnetic north, the opposite direction of refrigerator magnets. If you look up, the North Star will be in your vernal equinox, right next to Uranus.

In late season, bucks will rub on the run, which may cause a big buck to get hung up in the branches of low trees, inflicting severe whiplash or even hanging them on the spot, making them much easier to skin.

In an area with lots of bucks, there is considerable one-upsmanship. Competing bucks rub higher than the previous headgear, like hands on a baseball bat. If you see two footprints next to a tree and a very high rub, a very aggressive buck (or an un-hobbled giraffe on a game preserve) is nearby.

WHERE DEER LIVE

IN THE MOUNTAINS:

SADDLES

FLATS

SOUTHERN EXPOSURE:

ELSEWHERE:

On the Edges of Habitat

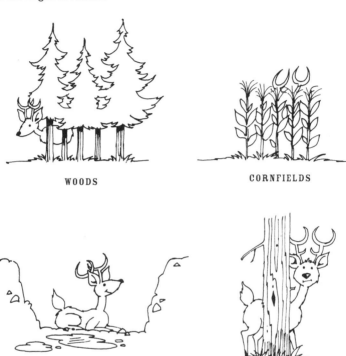

WOODS

CORNFIELDS

ALONG RIVER BOTTOMS

BEHIND TREES

HOW THEY TRAVEL

Deer traditionally move in groups and all share similar configurations.

The group will always be formed into a V, patterned after their flying feathered friends. During the hunting season, the inner V will be centered with the big buck as shown below. The fawns are too young to be aware of their role in the formation.

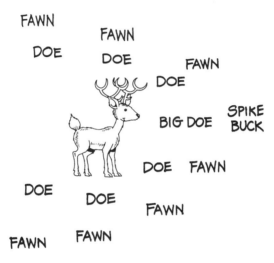

FAWN

FAWN

DOE   DOE

FAWN

DOE

BIG DOE   SPIKE BUCK

DOE   FAWN

DOE   DOE

FAWN

FAWN   FAWN

MIGRATIONS AND REASONS

CHANGE OF FOODS: When winter hits with high snows that cover the groceries, deer will move to lower elevations for super-sized portions.

CHANGE OF SEASONINGS: When road crews put too much salt on their roadside snacks, deer move from the asphalt to country dirt roads.

CHANGE OF WEATHER: Less known is the movement of midwestern deer that don't want to spend another cold winter up north. Only the ones who can't afford the trip are condemned to starve in the deeryards of Minnesota and Wisconsin. Before the first big storm, travelers group along the state borders north of Chicago and east of Minneapolis, and follow the major interstates south, taking care to avoid all population centers and traveling at night. Truck drivers have spotted them when they aren't all able to squeeze into the road culverts. The exact routes are unknown. The ones who head in a westerly direction prefer the Scottsdale area for year-round golf. The snowbirds heading east by southeast most likely visit their dwarf cousins in the Florida Keys.

WHERE THEY SLEEP

WHAT YOU THINK THEIR BEDS LOOK LIKE:

WHAT THEY REALLY LOOK LIKE:

Depending on the size of the animal, deer beds are six to eight feet long, dug down into a hollow and surrounded by their favorite twigs, berries, leaves, and left-behind hunter apparel. Since most does have twin fawns, you'll see many twin-size beds. They graduate to larger beds as necessary, beds having a double role as sleep and frolic area. The king of the herd has his own size bed and the queen hers. Early in a courtship, one bed will be left cold overnight. If they have been together for a long time, these beds move further apart. California deer, while not any larger than others, tend to have longer beds due to what biologists describe as a need for more space.

When deer lie down, does and spike bucks will lie flat, changing sides nightly so one side will not become flatter than the other. Pregnant does find sleeping uncomfortable in any position and will sleep on their backs, with their legs straight up and slightly folded at the knee. Big bucks have a more difficult time sleeping with their big rack of antlers. A buck's bed will have a hollow at one end where his rack can rest. Restless bucks sleep like horses, leaning against a tree if they have been out all night, and sport hunters can shoot away the tree and let the fall take its toll. Some deer sleep with just their head up and eyes closed. Others sleep with their eyes open, but it's really hard on the surface of the eyeballs. You can identify these deer by how often they have to blink.

Young deer sleep the night through and play all day. Older deer try to snooze in the day and do their deer duties at night when hunters are drunk in their sleeping bags. It's not known if deer dream but old-timers claim to have heard deer snore, especially the big bucks who have just finished a large meal of dirt-covered acorns, washed down with fresh, giardia-infused stream water.

Deer sleep where they feel safe. As deer communities are compressed by the scorched earth policies of developers and national park rangers, game biologists have identified two typical patterns of bedding.

A CROWDED URBAN COMMUNITY

Population specialists have found entire families living on just one side of the main trail. The family beds are the sites of all the animal reunions. The more troublesome bucks spend the early evenings at the major trail junctions, often up to no good.

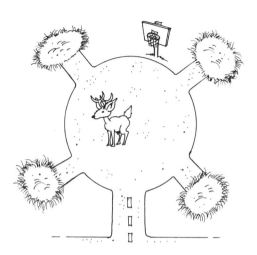

A CROWDED SUBURBAN COMMUNITY

Deer "burbs" are separated from the more concentrated populations by a river, lake, or railroad tracks. The dominant animals live here, with more pronounced social habits and guest quarters. The beds with water frontage are most prized. The best-looking does mate with the bucks from these neighborhoods. These females are less faithful, and will slip along a back trail between the legs of a bachelor buck should her resident male be away for an extended period of time. Bucks bed with the wind to their backs, facing the driveway. The backyard is never trimmed the way it should be and always faces deep cover. Beds on hillsides rank second in popularity, especially with a view of doe areas or hunting camps.

EATING HABITS

Learn the regular habits of your quarry and no habit is more regular than a deer grubbing for food. If you've done your homework, you'll recognize the half-digested foods inside your critter's gut pile. There are three distinct types of foodstuffs: what they prefer to eat, what their parents taught them to eat, and what will keep them alive.

WHAT THEY EAT: In the woods, deer browse on leaves, buds, and soft twigs in the spring. A preferred food is the wild mushroom cap stuffed with wild berries. When the leaves turn color, deer reach for elm, cedar, white pine, and dogwood twigs, and bend over for sassafras and poison ivy. A favorite is acorns, which are also high on the ground squirrel's list. In hard times, old-timers have reported wallhangers chasing ground squirrels for a large nut.

On the flatlands, young wild grasses and cash crops like wheat and cannabis are staple items in a deer's diet. Fruit and peanuts are an animal's fast food. Deer love sweet corn. Holding the ear between both front feet they eat it as they've been taught, across the row, end to end. In Carter country, deer eat goobers, with the accompanying bad breath. Whitetails eat all vegetables but have difficulty persuading the fawns to finish their Brussels sprouts.

On the mountains, mulies prefer a diet of bitterbrush, rabbit brush, mountain mahogany, ceanothus, and cannabis.

Urban deer gorge on the decorative shrubs found around large condo projects. This rich diet must be combined with other, even more nutritious grains.

WHEN THEY EAT: Deer prefer to eat at night when they are out of the crosshairs of some bushwhacker. The problem is that they can't see what they are eating, so a stalker will notice lots of spit-up food from night feeders. If the animals must eat during the more dangerous day, they do so on their knees. This is very uncomfortable and lying down makes it no more difficult to swallow.

HOW THEY EAT: Except for two upper front teeth, deer have to gum their food. Deer nibble like a suburban housewife at a food fair. Under pressure, deer gulp their food with predictable indigestion. Deer need roughage and eat the hard grains because they feel it's good for them.

WHERE THEY EAT: You can tell where deer are browsing by noticing the feeding lines on trees:

Fawns have a difficult time getting above the browse line and must stand on top of each other to have dinner.

TOILET HABITS

Deer go toilet more often than humans, especially number one. Bucks go to relieve bladder pressure and mark their territory, much like a bass fisherman during a backyard Beer-B-Que. They urinate standing in their own scrapes, in less dominant deer's scrapes, and on smaller sleeping bucks.

Does like to pee together and will do so ten to fifteen times a day. Large groups of does will potty together. These doe potty areas are much messier than buck biffies and much easier to find. It's almost like the does don't care about the cleanliness of these areas.

Does squat like a dog, the more experienced raising their tail before going. There are no reports of co-ed toileting. Oldtimers have spotted young bucks lurking around doe toilets, hoping to catch a peek of a lifted tail. This behavior really irritates the matriarchs, even though the younger does seem flattered by the attention.

All deer must go Big Job, or number two, on a regular basis or experience gastric distress. No matter where they live, their diet must be properly balanced with roughage, water, and a sweet now and then for regularity. Deer scat is an important indicator of general living activity and full of clues for successful hunting. If the scat is cold and hard, the deer sign is old. If the scat is warm and moist, the deer might be around the next bend, so be ready. If the little pellets are hot with just a little crust, be careful as you raise your head. Pellets are oval shaped so the back door doesn't slam shut each time, and come in designer colors from taupe to light camel. To find out what your prized buck is eating, break open a pellet for samples. Crack open with your fingers, or if difficult, with your freshly whitened dentures. You may see seeds, twigs, Fritos, or, if you are real lucky, your fortune in each pellet.

ANIMAL SEX

Sex as practiced by large animals has been a lively subject of study by a subspecies of biologist. These sex specialists have spent countless sleepless nights watching deer doing the deed and come to exhibit animal-like behavior in their own boudoir.

The deer's favored position is dog-style. During the act, a buck barks like a dog and changes to a howl toward the end. A large buck will reach up and put his feet over the doe's eyes, adding a little mystery to what in an established relationship could become stale.

Is there truly safe sex among deer? Yes, if done according to conservative recommendations. Frequently there is the innocent passing of mites or body crabs, but there seems to be no social stigma attached. Only in established herds is there any evidence of deviant sex, and then only among deer that hang around drive-in movies and shopping malls.

Like most old-church Catholic women, deer do not practice effective birth control and their reckless disregard has resulted in the deer population explosion and subsequent expanded seasons and game limits. It's their own fault. Draw extra doe permits and fill them.

THE RUT: In late summer or early fall when the lights begin to dim, bucks enter a period of their life called the rut. Life in the rut is a time of single-focus activity, a lot like a sailor on shore leave. The male fluids collect forward and build pressure from the groin, ending with a swollen neck. In severe cases, the essential juices push up into the head, whiting out the normally dark eyes. During this time a buck becomes a four-legged love muscle, raping and pillaging like a Norseman. This condition comes with a pubescent odor, a sweet smell normally associated with the vicar's private study.

Bucks normally service six to ten does each during the rut. The big bucks get the best does. The young ones have to wait until they are three to four years old, roughly middle age in human years before they can have their first lick.

Does are normally very receptive while in heat, or estrus. This honeymoon period lasts about twenty-four to thirty-six hours every twenty-eight days between October and December, and some does can have up to three heats in a single season. While she is in heat, a doe will seem to shy away from bucks, hiding her bush behind a bush, and even sitting on her powder puff while at the same time flirting and searching for the best buck in the animal kingdom.

A buck sniffs doe buffs on regular rounds and if one is in heat, the buck will nuzzle a bit, and make false deer promises to be faithful and a good provider. Some bucks bring presents of chewed-up acorns. At this point, the receptive doe will be overcome with emotion. Then they "do it." Bucks "do"a doe in five to six seconds, which seems about right. Once "it's" finished, the buck leaves to talk over the latest conquest with the other bucks. The done doe will not be receptive to any junior bucks looking for seconds.

After the rut, the most active bucks lose weight, become scraggly-looking, and get ready to lose their antlers, leaving them truly boneless.

MATING: Read the story of Bambi real close and you'll glean the disgusting fact that Bambi not only married his first cousin, Faline, but rutted with her and had children, too. Similar to the sad tales of the British monarchy and incestuous relationships that produced extra long backbones on idiots, this family inbreeding is what first produced tails on deer and is considered by the herd's religious leaders as evidence of original sin. Look close at the pictures of Noah's Ark and you'll see just tail stubs. There are certain parts of the country, like in the back hills of North Carolina and Georgia, where this sort of thing has been going on for a long time. Local old-timers report seeing older deer with elongated tails, having a hard time getting it up. They have been seen to step on that thick appendage when walking backwards, and fall down to the catcalls of other woodland friends. Their tails naturally erase tracks making these trophies difficult to hunt.

Does choose mates who are winners. They look for a young buck on the move, preferably from a good family, and with good health and skin, a pitch-black nose, and strong lower back teeth. Some does select the sleeker males with well-defined musculature and smaller butts. Other does prefer the mature animal knowing their personalities are more evenly balanced and they don't spend all the daylight hours preening at trail crossings. Other does opt for the safety of the trophy buck harems and are thought to be more submissive. In the genetic lore book passed down from generation to generation, these does are usually offshoots from a transcontinental migration of mixed whitetail and mule deer that left the woodlands of the Midwest under an unexplained habitat stress and are the nucleus of the large harems found in Utah.

Scientific studies have isolated four new mating behavior patterns:

✔ *OLDER BUCK/PREEMIE DOE:* These lolitas of the woods loiter near the stage doors of the stag area, squealing like groupies and bleating for a little eye contact. A buck in midlife crisis may take a young one under its horn. Herd social leaders publicly disapprove but privately yearn for this activity.

✔ *YOUNG BUCK/OLDER DOE:* Led astray by an older but still attractive female, the young buck is quickly taught the mysteries of the woods. A wise doe knows how to rub a buck the right way.

✔ *CROSSING THE SPECIES LINE:* Generally speaking, whitetail deer will not mate with mule deer. They consider their western cousins coarse and brutish. When the herds rub together, there is little or no flirting and only adolescent rebels cross the line.

✔ *BUCK/COW:* Only a buck overdosed on hormones will hump a Holstein. On rare occasions, a longhorn will teach a whitetail doe a few rough lessons in animal sex.

HAVING CHILDREN: Like farm girls, deer breed in the fall and birth in the spring. The gestation period is about six months long, and all the forest creatures celebrate the birth of a fawn.

A healthy, well-fed doe will have at least one if not two fawns at a time. There are rare but increasingly more frequent occurrences of multiple births, associated with the consumption of genetically engineered, fast-growing "super" grasses. Deer having quintuplets stay dazed for a full year and lose interest in sex. The doe is finally able to stand again after six months. She will carry a grudge against the buck that put her in that condition and shy away from the deer social events that led her to trouble in the first place.

Birthing is in May and June and a fawn will weigh about four pounds (or about a pound and a half of camp meat). The buck will never be around to help when needed. Friends of the doe will attend to the needs of the new mother.

The little fawns keep their spots and long lashes until September, and are breastfed until the bucks push them away during the rut. Fawns stay with the does as long as they can but grow up without a strong male role model. This leads to identity problems for the younger bucks.

GROWING UP IN A TROUBLED WORLD

The fawns' first shock is the forced landing on the forest floor. The second slap is the reality of a demanding deer world. Deer daycare centers are organized to help busy adult deer raise their offspring. From the first days in these remote centers, fawns learn how to lift their tails, twitch their ears, keep their eyes moist, and chew with their mouths closed.

Most experts say deer stay in their home territory of a square mile or so. That may be so for those stay-at-home whitetails, but generally speaking, deer are no different than humans. Adolescents will get goosey and roam up to ten miles, and the more adventurous hop across a state line or border for a night. Young bucks avoid fighting with the old man this way and the more promiscuous does escape the domestic chores of the bedding area.

As adults, deer must cope with the geometrically increasing sophistication of the modern hunter, the growing ranks of the trophy hunter, and acid rain. Only the strong can survive in the post-nuclear woods and deer have no break in sight, no light at the end of the tunnel. There is hope in states like Wisconsin where deer are not seriously disturbed during the hunting season. There is chatter within the Zoological Society about turning that entire state into a national zoo. Early political test balloons, especially those flown in Minnesota, have shown a positive response.

VETERAN DEER

Survivors of multiple seasons hold reunions after each one closes, next to the hunter parking lots. The veterans compare notes with the young bucks listening in, and the does prepare large meals of whole grains, berries, and mast. All the latest tricks are discussed: current camo, scents, deer stands, and changes in regulations. Small memorial piles of acorns mark empty places around the circle. Until everyone has a chance to get to the reunion, there is quite a bit of concern about attendance. Those animals with arrows still stuck in their haunches have them bitten off by more junior animals with stronger teeth.

The season's best stories are told in a complicated series of grunts and bleats, and often accompanied by what sounds like chuckles, especially from areas with a high proportion of non-resident hunters.

Deer are normally very imitative. Noting the increased hunter use of mock scrapes and rubs, the veteran deer describe their use of mock beds and trails to the yearlings. Pawing the outline of the area in the dirt, the seniors show where they plan to walk backwards next season and in which inaccessible area to build their mock beds. The elders show spike bucks how to walk in moose tracks. Mule deer show how to imitate whitetail by lifting the flag and hopping like a rabbit. Whitetails explain how to "mock-mule" by walking ten yards and turning around, walking ten yards and turning around. The veterans discuss the fashionable methods of hunting and recount late into the evening memories of the worst cases of buck fever.

THE
HUNTER

TYPES OF HUNTERS

The many types of hunters share basic hunting desires and are easily distinguished from one another.

THE TROPHY HUNTER will pass up better eating does for a mangy old buck whose head will fit on the trophy wall, and talk with magnum muzzles about their quest for the largest headgear. Their trophy scores are kept in some big book somewhere. Trophy hunters shoot trophy guns, wear trophy clothing, and have exclusively trophy hunting experiences. Without a trophy-sized listening audience, these hunters atrophy and their trophy wives often move on to a more target-rich environment.

THE ORDINARY HUNTER is a regular guy, scratching to get out of the house and away from the old lady and the "shitlins" for a few days, and putting his boss' face on an unsuspecting animal.

THE ACCIDENTAL HUNTER acquires an animal by bumper-kissing Bambi off a byway or by accidentally firing a rifle out a car window into a well-lit herd of night-feeders.

THE NON-RESIDENT HUNTER wants to be a local good old boy and will do anything to bag your deer. They are identified by new gear. Each day in camp, they wait for an overnight delivery of new catalog items for any late-breaking hunting strategy. In the local taverns, non-residents are quickly under the influence, and can be counted on to start at least one bar fight and dance with the ugliest women.

THE CITY HUNTER is an escapee from a sissy white-collar cubicle job, is terrified he will do something wrong, and makes a good camp girl.

THE RESIDENT HUNTER is recognized solely by his generosity to the non-residents.

PRESEASON ACTIVITY

MENTAL PREPARATIONS: Before you go tromping in the woods with dangerous weapons, Buck recommends multiple trips to the local zoo to see what a real deer looks like. Note the docile animals playing deer games. They seem very content and well fed, and happy to walk around in large circles. Disregard the dead-deer-walking look in their eyes.

Movies are a good way to get to know your animal. The Disney classic, *Bambi*, has produced generations of camp meat hunters, and neighborhood theaters will often show great nature films on Saturdays at matinee rates. You can discover Mother Nature on many cable channels, narrated by khaki-clad, talking trophy heads. Rarely do you see the animals being skinned in the barn or the femurs being chewed by stray dogs.

Prepare for a deer encounter by purchasing a plastic deer for your yard. Get a full-size one that looks like the real thing as you drive real fast, practicing road hunting. It's one more way for the neighbors to know you appreciate Mother Nature. The statues add class to the front of a house but are more functional in the backyard where you can play wilderness games without being distracted by neighborhood crazies or policemen.

Realistic wall coverings are available that show deer in natural settings. These full-size, four-color photographs bring the wild to you in the comfort of your own living or dining room. Find a trophy head at an antique store to hang in your bedroom. It's very important to fix these deer images in your mind at least three to six months before the season begins.

EQUIPMENT: It's not much fun to hunt without the right gear. Your friends will laugh at you. You won't be able to shoot a deer either. During preseason, buy and try out all of the right new gear to make sure everything fits and works properly.

Three months before the season, estimate what you'll weigh and buy clothes to fit the new you. Foot and hand sizes stay the same unless you work at the mill or in a restaurant kitchen.

Buck recommends wearing new gear, especially camo gear, on trips to the zoo to see if the deer recognize you. The gear may make you a little warm during the early summer months, but it's a good test to see if the miracle fabrics will wick away moisture as promised. Wear the clothes while working in the backyard and call your little lady out on the back step to see if she can spot you. Wear your boots as often as you can. Like many commuters who wear walking shoes to the train, wear your Sorels and change into work shoes at the office.

Wear your new gear outside to air out the store-bought smells. Some of Buck's buddies bury their new gear in the backyard for a month or so, then get a few gallons of swamp water from their hunting grounds and convince a new hunting partner to wash the gear with this natural water in his wife's washing machine when she is not home. This technique really sets the clothes up nice. If you add some heavier dirt and twigs, the clothes soften to become high fashion stonewashed togs.

Early in the fall, start gathering the old clothes for each upcoming season. Buck finds the most convenient way is to build piles of equipment in a handy place, like a hallway or sewing room, by season—one for duck hunting, one for deer hunting—capping the pile with the appropriate headgear. When the season is over, return the used clothing to the same location for your spouse's easy handling.

WEAPONS TRAINING: Get to know your gun early. Buck says a man who doesn't know his gun is not his kind of man. Take the firearm apart in daylight, at night, and in your bed. Take the firearm to work disassembled and reassemble during boring sales meetings. Focus your scope (unattached to the firearm unless your company allows high-powered rifles in worker's cubicles) at inanimate things like your boss or supervisor, or the more animate frisky items in the upstairs bedroom window next door. You'll notice the more powerful scopes can pick up very interesting low-light activity.

The worst thing about shooting a gun is the noise and felt recoil. Get used to loud noises before you practice at the range. Celebrate your purchase of a new firearm during Chinese New Year in the International District and you'll know what opening day in Wisconsin sounds like. Have your wife sneak up on you and pop balloons whenever and wherever you least expect, particularly in the early and late hours of the day.

Your heavy hunting clothes absorb most of the recoil from high-caliber rifles. Buy commercial recoil pads or have them built into your jacket. They always look goofy on just one side and padded on both sides, you'll look like a non-resident. Rip out the shoulder pads from a dress in your lady's closet you never liked and strap them to your body with Ace bandages. Heavy recoil can be prepared for by shooting that new elephant gun at the rifle range with only your shirt on. This method will toughen those recoil muscles. If you are a bow hunter, put blunt ends on your arrows and pop off a couple at the zoo. It won't hurt the animals. And creates that dangerous environment that they miss. If they had a brain.

METHODS OF HUNTING: Buck recommends practicing your style of hunting. If you are a crawler, creep up on Ol' Blue death rattling through his last sleep in the backyard, circling to keep downwind, and goose him when he's least expecting.

If you stand hunt, practice-sit in a makeshift stand at home. If you have a loft or second-floor balcony, sit up there a full day, and watch your little lady walk below. Perch outside in a favorite tree or on the roof and watch the neighborhood. Wear your new camo gear but it's more prudent to practice this technique in the backyard. Spend a full quiet day there with a packed lunch and carry on as you would in deep timber. Build your own stand near well-traveled neighborhood trails. Remember that you are already near suspected bedding areas. Note any patterns of behavior. You may have several domestic pets join you, but never mind.

If you are a stalker, start shadowing your animal rights activist neighbor's wife as she walks to the supermarket. She will follow a familiar trail and is easily tracked in the neighborhood's natural terrain. The red high heels that make her calves so shapely leave easy tracks. Like her woodland counterpart, she will probably stop along the way to browse. Give her leeway unless you want to see how skittish does get when threatened. These does can call a badge.

At the office, start on the scent trail of that blonde the boss hired. You are in full camouflage and the tracking will not seem any different from any other major office activity. Stand near the water cooler and the major runways adjacent to elevators or potty areas. Get as close to her bedding area as possible.

If you are a ground sitter, practice sitting absolutely still on the floor of the family room occasionally watching all directions for unusual movement but concentrating on the sports channel. Test the latest electronic earmuffs to soften your wife's good suggestions and still allow you to hear the game. Avoid all eye contact with your loved ones. Deer consider direct eye contact very aggressive and impolite. Sharpen your hearing by sitting under your neighbor's bedroom window, listening for unusual noises.

If you expect Lady Luck to smile on your first hunt, work on dragging skills. Practice dragging your wife across a yard full of obstacles on a plastic sheet. If you expect to hunt in real cold weather, take long naps in your walk-in freezer.

Preseason hunting is an excellent way to sharpen your large animal skills. Unless you hunt deer that fly, bird hunting is only good for your shotgunning skills. That's no reason not to go anyway. An excellent preseason quarry is the wily gray squirrel. They have quick reflexes, fine senses, live in the woods, and can be hunted with rifles that are easy on your ears. They scamper about the woods and can fine-tune your hearing as they scream squirrel obscenities from treetops. They can sharpen your eyesight by flashing small BA's before diving down a tree hole. If you are going to hunt from a tree stand, make sure you have a ground partner or dog to chase them up your tree. Imagine the look on their faces as they race up the branch that happens to be your leg. On those occasions, pray they've had their daily ration of nuts. Imagine the look on your face if they haven't.

Prepare your special part of the woods for a productive hunt. Make it easier for deer to get to your stand by bringing in a backhoe and carving out a path for your friends. The larger and wider you make it, the more deer will use it. If you make it wide enough, you'll see whole families, with fawns frolicking out front, and does chatting about common deer household things and thick-necked, horny bucks not far behind.

Preseason preparations include bringing in salt licks and fruit and vegetable displays. Since deer like salt, there is reason to think they will like other seasonings such as pepper.

A herd decoyed like this is easy to track due to the sneezing.

BUCK'S BONUS TIP: Once you think you have your preseason hunting legs, go to the hunting shows in full gear, sporting a name you made up for yourself, like "Mule Deer Mike." Walk by the big displays of mounted heads saying loudly, "Yeah, I have (fill in number) of those on my wall." Tell guides you have so many heads registered in Boom and Crockpot or Poop and Young you must hunt under an alias. Don't spend a lot of time with the guides representing hunting camps because they are not really interested in helping you hunt anyway, and are only there to hustle city women with shaved legs. If you return on the second day of the show, look for love marks on their necks.

HUNTING WIDOWS

The oft-forgotten member of the deer hunting family is the lovely spouse, the old lady, the little woman. Hunters' wives suffer quietly through the preseason preparations; the emergency budgeting for those secret withdrawals from the joint checking account; and the long smoky, beery planning sessions in the family room. She bemoans her fate when she and millions like her become hunting widows during the deer season. As their husbands back out of the driveway, they take their lonely posts in the upper windows and await their man's return. Either that or race out the back door to service the lawn boy, or for that matter, any male—the gardener, the postman, the village idiot on the park bench.

Like widows who have recently lost a wealthy but aged husband, hunting widows have short bereavements and usually recover by early evening to put on a new dress and head for the hottest bistro in town. There they bask in the adoration of non-hunting Italians and other Latins, all of whom dance better than that oaf in the woods. During breaks in the music, the lovely legions of the abandoned swear blood oaths of secrecy, and arrive home in time to shower the stink off and smile out the kitchen window at the meat wagon pulling up the driveway. And just call for more lawn service in the morning.

CHOOSING YOUR HUNTING PARTNER

The second most important decision you'll make in your life (second only to the caliber of rifle to buy) is your choice of hunting partner or partners. Your best hunting buddy can share your dreams, your plans, and your table, and if quarters are tight, your bed too. For all these reasons, stay away from complainers, game hogs, and lazy out-of-condition bums. This eliminates your in-laws and other dickwads.

HUNTING WITH A WOMAN: The gentle sex has built-in advantages in that they are more intuitive and have better senses than you. A good woman can detect imitation scents on another woman, spot the differences between zircons and diamonds, and overhear gossip that can cripple a career.

✔ *A GIRLFRIEND:* This is one dear heart you want to capture, so show her what makes you tick. A trip into the woods might just seal the deal, and then again might not.

✔ *YOUR WIFE:* You are on dangerous ground here. Can she appreciate your efforts by actually watching them?

✔ *YOUR SECRETARY:* The prudes down in Human Resources advise not to "dip your pen in the company inkwell," but there is no better mentoring opportunity than in a deer stand built for one but occupied by two.

✔ *A CAMP WIFE FROM LAS VEGAS:* A smart choice. Card tricks are only one of many they can turn for you.

HUNTING WITH FAT PEOPLE: In addition to their overwhelming presence at the camp dinner table, people with low muscle mass need steel and concrete reinforced tree stands, tire too easily while driving deer, and usually eat their lunch before mid-morning. They are more sensitive and make good camp girls, although they use too much hot water during their showers.

HUNTING WITH SKINNY PEOPLE: Going back to biblical (even Roman) times thin people are not to be completely trusted. They are no good in a bar fight and can't pull out a deer under their own power. Their shoulders are too thin to absorb the recoil of a high-powered rifle and they spend the entire night rubbing Ben-Gay into their bed sheets. You can't borrow clothes from them and they have feet like women. They do camo well but their high-pitched voices can empty a target-rich environment.

HUNTING WITH DIVORCED PEOPLE: Hunting buddies with wandering wives suffer two ways. Either they have been emasculated by the divorce court and lost all primal urges and would rather just sit and sob under an oak tree, or they have regained their stuff and become overaggressive, shooting more female deer than the law allows.

HUNTING WITH DISABLED PEOPLE: In most states, the handicapped are the only ones who can shoot from a motorized vehicle. The current interpretation is "physically" handicapped and avoids the whole mental issue. Have your chair-bound buddy power up to cruise the roads while you're driving deer out of their beds. A large chair with a towrope is handy for dragging, too.

HUNTING WITH THE VISUALLY IMPAIRED: Responsible Wisconsin state senators have finally passed a bill that allows people to hunt who present medical evidence that they are unable to hunt alone because of blindness. This legislation was a compromise between the lobbies for the blind drunk and the just plain blind. Under this bill, a blind person can hunt and shoot if accompanied by a sighted hunter. The only requirement is that the rifle be painted white with a red barrel tip. The rifles are also outfitted with double sights and triggers similar to a driver's education car. Once the animal is within "sight," the regular hunter taps the blind hunter on the back of the head to shoot. Each time an animal is missed, the tap gets to be more like a slap. There is no clear limit on how many blind people you can take into the woods with you. Until all this is straightened out, Buck will not be hunting in Wisconsin.

HUNTING WITH CANADIANS: These sort-of-English-speaking people are required in most bordering states to hunt in pairs, one to carry and aim the gun, the other to yell, "Shoot!" They are highly irritable at being pulled away from televised hockey games and need help dressing in the morning in order to keep the zippers and buttons facing forward. With their gun laws, many Canadians are reduced to hunting with hockey sticks over maple sugar licks.

HUNTING WITH EUROPEANS: The more violent Southern Europeans are best suited for blood sports, and if they can turn their guns away from their incessant family feuds long enough, they are good hunters. They are familiar with stuffing large dead things in trunks and long disposed to using weapons to settle domestic disputes.

Northern Europeans traditionally turn their guns on themselves, particularly during the long cold winters. If a purebred Norwegian is hunting with you and you hear a shot, assume an empty seat at the camp dinner table. It's difficult for just one Scandinavian to put the long barrel of a muzzleloader into his mouth, but no problem with the help of a close relative. At the rifle ranges in Norway, range masters don't even set targets. In Sweden, more bullets are needed because of near misses even at that close range. In Finland, wives and any member of her family eagerly volunteer to pull the trigger. Scandinavians are raised to exhibit enthusiasm for nothing and it's only on occasional lutefisk overdoses that their billfolds will actually leave the baggy pants to buy a friend a cup of coffee. Germans really enjoy shooting at anybody, particularly the French, but only after a big greasy meal washed down by kiloliters of warm beer. The French will hunt but only cut out the filets and leave the rest to rot, and then cover the filets with some horrid sauce.

SPECIAL "DIANA THE HUNTRESS" SECTION

Buck has gone to considerable expense to research the habits of the woman hunter. He has left no stone under one carat unturned and this is what he has learned.

Woman has always been the hunter. The Greeks knew that first, then the editors of *Cosmopolitan*. The hunting skills of the lioness are the pride of the pride. Have you ever witnessed the opening hour of a women's shoe sale? You'll understand.

Women hunters will not shoot fawns unless they have a baby with colic at home. Career women prefer to blast does. If a female hunter becomes a trophy buck hunter, it's an indication of trouble at home or a blocked career path.

WARNING: If accepted in your hunting party, your woman will let her body hair grow out. She has always wanted to so make sure she shaves once home or next she'll buy a Subaru and sing "I am woman, hear me roar" in the shower.

LIFE IN CAMP

The different kinds of camp are directly related to the state of the bank account at the time of planning. There is an evolutionary scale of camps, but there are two basic types: outdoors or indoors, with or without a hard roof, or, as your woman carries on, with or without facilities. Buck has tried them all and describes how your choices affect your hunting day:

OUTDOOR CAMPS

✔ *ON THE GROUND:* J. Angus "Sourdough" McLean has laid a bag in many a hollow but dislikes sharing his nuts with the ground squirrels. Avoid damp creek beds, sloped land, and caves with traces of bear breath. The single advantage of a ground camp is that it can be turned into a ground stand.

✔ *LEAN-TO:* A temporary shelter at best, a lean-to is essentially a roof fashioned from tarp, canvas, a jacket, branches, or an old car door held up with rope, twine, or your belt. A lean-to can make for fitful sleeping. A cold, damp lean-to can make for fitful sleeping. Like your sleeping bag. And easy for a bear to enter.

INDOOR CAMPS

✔ *CABIN:* What you'd build as a hunting camp if you ran out of money halfway through, substituting linoleum for hardwood, and chintz for drapes, and installing no-name "damaged" appliances. The mattresses are purchased from motel bankruptcy proceedings and pillows are stuffed with packing popcorn.

✔ *MOTEL:* Distinguished by harvest gold shag carpeting and pole lamps. The front door is two giant steps from your front bumper. The more expensive motels have their own coffeemakers and sanitized paper strips across the toilet seats. The less expensive have alarm clocks checked out at the office and a pay phone on the parking lot light pole. The mattresses are purchased from hotel bankruptcy proceedings and pillows are stuffed with cork.

✔ *HOTEL:* If you are staying at a hotel, you are either not hunting or hunting dears. The mattresses are freshly turned and pillows are stuffed with shredded complaint cards.

✔ *LODGE:* Reserved for the Fortune 500, these hunting heavens must only be taken in small doses. Many of Buck's friends have stopped hunting after overexposure to lodge creature comforts. The mattresses are covered with camouflage-patterned protectors and pillows are stuffed with your choice of grouse, chukar, or turkey feathers.

Your choice of camp type will affect your behavior:

	OUTDOOR CAMPS	INDOOR CAMPS
TOILET	Not allowed in sleeping bag.	On pot, according to seniority.
EATING	Hot foods over a fire. Cold foods in the bag.	If with a woman, in all the rooms.
SLEEPING	In the bag, if you can.	As assigned by elders.
DRINKING	In the bag, in the bag.	Everywhere.
LYING, BOASTING, AND CHEATING	Both inside and outside the bag.	Everywhere.
PUKING	In someone else's bag.	Out the window, out the door, just out!

The hunting camp is a happy camp, free of domestic and professional concerns. Responsibilities are minor and easily managed within the hunting hierarchy.

✔ *THE SENIOR HUNTERS,* called Stags, have at least seven seasons and seven animals (five bucks) under their belts, and are entitled to:

Sleep in single beds and get any extra blankets and pillows.

Turn in the earliest and sleep in the latest.

Get their choice of camp meats.

Have camp coffee fixed their way.

Belch at the table.

Have priority seating on toilets.

Hunt a day or so but may stay longer.

Say "This food tastes like garbage!"

✔ *THE SOON-TO-BE-SENIORS,* called the Velvets, have at least five seasons and five animals (four bucks) to their credit and can:

Sleep in a double bed and get one extra pillow.

Be the first to say goodnight to the seniors.

Set the alarm clocks and inspect kitchen.

Belch outside.

Follow on the warm toilet seat vacated by a Stag.

Hunt extra days to fill out the camp bag.

Say "This food is a tad greasy."

✔ *THE INTERMEDIATES,* called Spike Bucks, have at least three seasons and three animals (two bucks), and must:

Sleep four to a queen-size bed, five to a king.

Bring own extra pillows and blankets.

Pay deposits on cabin.

Hold belch and gas until well into the woods.

Eat what everybody else eats.

Hunt until they kill their own deer.

Say "This food is a little cold."

✔ *THE JUNIORS*, called the Buckettes, are working up the ladder, aren't distinguished by season or animals and are required to:

> Do all the dishes, drag out the deer, and dig latrines.
> Sleep on floor if available.
> Arrive first, wake up first, and make coffee to order.
> Brasso the bullets of the seniors.
> Eat what the senior hunters recommend.
> Hunt only as long as their seniors say they can.
> Say "This food is not bad."

✔ *THE FIRST-TIMERS*, called Bambos, are the responsibility of the Juniors and must be seen, not heard. They are not allowed to have live ammunition and cannot eat until everyone else has had their fill. They will be the butt of many camp pranks. A common refrain: "Is there any food left?"

Buck prefers hunting from camps that come with kitchens opening into living rooms with TVs connected to satellite dishes aimed at the Playboy channel.

FOOD IN THE CAMP: Indians prepared themselves for a hunt by fasting, hoping that self-discipline would make the animal gods reward their efforts with a big animal. The non-resident deer hunter's idea of fasting is refusing the last beer in someone else's cooler. Old-timers ate what the deer were eating: a bowl of acorns garnished with a sprig of honeysuckle for color, and washed down by river water. This spare diet reminded early hunters of the world of the deer but was soon abandoned once they learned how hard it was to pass those acorns, especially those with husk. Camp food is what your wife, mother, or daughter told you not to eat anyway. Food with high saturated fat. Burp. Excuse me! Frrrt! Whoops. That was a wet one.

FOOD IN THE WOODS: Nobody will know what you are eating, so all the things your whining old lady and family doctor have warned you about can be eaten in peace and quiet. There are basically two food groups.

✔ *FOOD TO FEED THE FURNACE:* All the baloney sandwiches in the world lie at your feet. They squash easily in your game bag and you can toss the crusts.

✔ *FOOD TO KEEP YOU MENTALLY ALERT:* If you are standing in a tree in Northern Minnesota all day long, have a supply of candy and dry snacks to chew on to keep you awake. A long day can be partially filled by unwrapping the more expensive items. Try to keep something in your mouth all day. If you are mentoring an outdoorswoman, this shouldn't be difficult.

THE CHURCH LUTEFISK DINNER

No deer season is complete without attending the annual hunter's lutefisk dinner. Normally held in the basement of the Lutheran church (or Catholic church if the Lutherans are not back from fishing), the annual fish feeds are a local food festival and out-of-town hunters are required to attend and eat all the lutefisk they can hold.

HOW TO EAT LUTEFISK

Pretend you have a cold and pack your nostrils with a piece of paper napkin or a spoonful of the crustier mashed potatoes. (It's not polite to pinch your nose.)

Swallow the smallest pieces as fast as you can.

Mash into the potatoes, though it is a shame to ruin good potatoes like that.

Hold chunks in your cheek and asked to be excused to go to the bathroom. If there is any room left in the toilet bowl, you can spit it all out.

Lutefisk sits in an esophageal purgatory halfway down your gullet while your stomach lining has a chance to hide all its sensitive nerve endings. If you jump around a lot during this period, you run the risk of seeing the fish again and the odds are it won't taste any better going down the second time. Once the Scandinavian seafood hits your stomach, it takes about seventy-two hours for the fish juices and your normal intestinal juices to get to know and dislike each other. The explosive mixture turns a still hunter into a driver.

THE MENU

ENTRÉE

LUTEFISK
In a butter sauce.   In a cream sauce.   In its own foul juices.

(*SWEDISH MEATBALLS* are offered to those who have a letter
from a doctor of at least one-half Scandinavian extraction
certifying a dangerous sensitivity to fishy traditions.)

SIDE DISHES

MASHED POTATOES in a big bowl with a small, deep
lake of butter in the middle and meatball gravy
as an afterthought.

CORN CASSEROLE with Rice Krispies® baked on top.

DINNER ROLLS with country butter and honey.

Lefse too, but too closely watched to steal some for the camp.

COFFEE and *MILK*. No alcohol. *CIDER*, maybe.

SETTLING INTO CAMP

PRESEASON PREPARATIONS: Start saving for your trip by secretly withdrawing funds from the joint checking account. Don't pack anything for the cabin that would give the little lady an excuse to buy something new for the house. Never let her go grocery shopping with you. Just tell her you'll pick up what you need on the day and once in the supermarket buy what you've been wanting to eat for the last year.

Listen to, but don't believe, the weather reports. A northerly wind to a meteorologist in a climate-controlled sound booth is the breeze of his secretary refreshing his coffee. Look for ice on the lake. Send a junior hunter to test its thickness. If he reports back dry as a bone, let him carry your backpack into the woods.

ARRIVAL INFORMATION: When you are unloading your gear, be sure to hide your best food. If you leave anything good out, the old-timers will bag it. Guaranteed!

Also hide your best long johns and socks. In every camp there are a few sorry individuals who never bring enough and they are the ones that have "accidents" in the woods.

CAMP MANNERS: If you are building a campfire outdoors, build it upwind of another camp's stand.

If you need to take your gun inside, unload it first. Unless you are going to play poker after dinner.

HUNTING TIPS: Once you've washed your body with odorless soap, dust yourself with baking soda or maybe it's baking powder. Buck doesn't remember which but one will keep you cool and dry.

In the last days of the season when hunters are slowing down, add a laxative in the breakfast eggs. The increased toilet activity might kick up an extra animal or two.

If you have been the butt of many practical jokes and are hunting a good distance from the others, shoot your deer, carry it out quickly and quietly along a different route, and go directly home. It'll make a long season for your buddies seem even longer.

DRINKING AND DEER HUNTING

Most states require deer hunters with drinking problems to wear blaze orange clothing. The laws vary from state to state, but there are mandatory percentages of clothing. The heaviest drinkers must wear more blaze orange than others. Some try unsuccessfully to hide their character flaws behind the new blaze orange camouflage.

There are a few ritual uses of liquor for a deer hunter. They are during:

The planning of the trip.
The night before leaving home.
The night before the hunt.
The first night of the hunt.
The last night of the hunt.
Any remaining nights of the hunt.
The first night at home.
Any remaining nights at home.

Drinking toasts are either congratulatory or commiserating, and offered by the senior members of the camp. They are as long as the attention span of the giver and about as interesting.

If you hunt in the backcountry of Georgia or North Carolina, you may run across an extra-legal liquor store hidden where the moon doesn't shine. Support the local economy. You were going blind anyway.

Buck does not drink while hunting as it's very difficult to keep a brandy warmer lit high in the stand.

HUNTING

METHODS OF HUNTING

STALKING DEER: An active hunt, which can be practiced by a single hunter.

✔ *CRAWLING* is the preferred way to sneak up on a deer, and the average crawler must cover over twenty miles a day to find a deer. Those miles are broken down into inches going over dead trees, through thorn and thistle, and around snake pits. There is no greater excitement, however, than crawling up on a deer snoozing in his or her bed, no greater surprise than when you fall into another camp's slit trench.

✔ *WALKING* is the most common way to stalk. A successful walker must walk cautiously and carefully, making as little noise as possible. Walk ten paces, then stop and listen. Stay clear of brush that will scratch your new gear and avoid stepping on big branches or fallen trees, no matter how much fun it is to hear them crack. Watch carefully for crawlers. If you do fall down, don't curse like you do at home. Walk on your toes like a deer. It's even better to move on all fours like the animal, moving slowly and stopping every so often as if you are having deer thoughts. While on your hands and knees, look under brush, low trees, and your back legs for deer legs.

If you have difficulty walking on all fours, walk with your buddy an arm's length apart, holding on his shoulders. The front person carries the weapon and is

responsible for shooting. Walk in synchronized steps, ten at a time, taking short stabbing steps like a ballerina. This technique is very effective, particularly in uncrowded woods, and can also help when you squire your little lady around the ballroom floor.

If while walking you see a deer out of the corner of your eye, keep walking. Do not look directly at the deer—they will bolt because of this aggressive behavior. Continue to walk calmly, mumbling about how you don't like to kill deer anyway, until out of sight when you can circle downwind and make them pay for their error in judgment.

✔ *POWERWALKING* is a less frequently observed technique and should be used only as a last resort, like when you finally realize nobody is looking for you. At that point, you might just as well moonwalk.

✔ *CHASING DEER* is an old Indian sport and initiation rite. The sport includes running down a young deer, trying to get close enough to hook an index finger into the critter's exhaust pipe and put on the brakes. This is not a pleasant experience for a mature buck. And real hard on your boot heels.

BUCK'S BONUS TIP: You can get too good at quietly stalking and scare the bejesus out of a very old buck snoozing away his remaining mornings. Break a twig, stop, and grunt every fifty yards or so. This will wake up the non-resident hunters, too.

STILL OR STAND HUNTING: Whether at ground level or at some elevation, still-hunting offers the purest forest experience. In a stand or blind, you can hear the cry of the whiffenpoof, the tap-tap-tap of the redheaded woodpecker, the scurry of the field mouse, and the sound of a hunting partner going grunt.

BUCK'S BONUS TIP: If that damn woodpecker keeps up that incessant tapping, chamber a light load and blow his pecker off.

Scandinavians excel in still-hunting as they are always pensively waiting for something good to happen. Hillbillies, especially offspring of first cousins, come in close second and the list winds down to the Southern Europeans like Italians who must be tightly strapped into tree stands due to their emotional outbursts.

In a stand, it's chicken one day and feathers the next, but the odds of bagging a deer from a stand are the highest of all lawful methods.

✔ *GROUND STANDS:* If you are afraid of heights, you'll have to choose between a natural or manmade ground stand. Natural stands include sitting against a tree stump or leaning against a rock formation. Buck prefers to use two special kinds of ground level stands.

The first uses the fact that a deer avoids making direct eye contact with a human and is easily stared down. This is embarrassing, especially for the larger deer, and the single most common cause of a white flag. Buck likes to hollow out a seat in the dirt that puts his chest just at ground level and cover his legs with debris and leaves. This stand puts the hunter below the deer's eye level and is effective in dry northern woods.

Buck's second most favorite stand has to do with a deer's diet. Deer really like apples, so one season Buck built a six-foot apple out of papier mâché, painted it red, and doused it with apple scents. Little piles of applesauce without cinnamon were scattered within fifty feet of this natural blind and deer came from miles around to view this natural wonder. When survivors gather around the old acorn pile, they still talk about that trip to the Big Apple. This noisy yet very effective stand only worked for one year and threw many deer off their normal feed, forcing Buck to switch to oversized pears and apricots in subsequent seasons.

Ground stands made by man are more varied, yet all share the common characteristic of being familiar to the deer.

✔ *THE AUTOMOBILE, TRUCK, OR CAMPER UNIT:* In Minnesota, a hunter with documented health issues can hunt from a parked vehicle but must roll down the window before shooting. Not so in Wisconsin.

> *BUCK'S BONUS TIP:* **Alert other occupants in the vehicle when you are about to pull the trigger so they can cover the dogs' ears.**

✔ *FISH HOUSES:* Why leave your two-holer in the backyard when it can serve two purposes? Normally equipped with only a small stove and a hard-backed chair, this stand is much like the home of a Norwegian bachelor and can keep you out of inclement weather.

There really is no reason why you couldn't pull in your bass boat as a stand. It has great seats and the multi-use will convince your wife of your economy. Deer in lake country are used to seeing bass boats.

✔ *PORTABLE TOILET STANDS:* These are Buck's favorite. They are pulled into the woods on skids by junior members of the camp and used units are not expensive, especially those used at rodeos. Take the door off and face toward the trail. With a two-holer, you can entertain guests.

✔ *TREE STANDS:* Most of these stands are put up into trees and are commercially made or homemade.

First, pick your tree. It should be located about fifty yards downwind of a scrape or fifty yards upwind of a non-resident hunter in prime habitat. Look at the tree like you would a woman. It will be naked by the time you use it, so pick trees that will hold their leaves or better yet pick a full, nicely sculpted tree so you can take it home after the hunt as a Christmas tree. Add festive spirit to the hunt by hanging a few red balls and some tinsel on your tree. Passing hunters who read children's books would think your display a modern miracle.

Second, it should be a live tree. If this live tree is on government land, you're not supposed to attach any permanent nails or stands. Then again, you're a taxpayer and if those high taxes don't earn you the right to pound a little nail, what will? Pick a tree with low growth so deer can feed right under you, allowing for that rare pituitary gland shot.

Third, your stand should be high enough to be above the prevailing ground winds that could blow your stink around the country. If it is too foggy to see the ground when you climb up into the stand, yet you can see small aircraft, you've gone too far. If you are hunting with a bow and arrow, an effective height is about twenty feet. With the longer range of a rifle, it's okay to go seventy feet or so. At that altitude, you'll enjoy goose migrations and the admiration of many a gray squirrel.

Fourth, strap yourself in for a good hunt. Many will use a strong, yet stretchy strap that allows the hunter to lean out from the tree to see what's coming up behind. Attach the strap below your neck and disconnect before you jump off the stand to go grunt.

✔ *MOBILE STANDS:* In Texas, there are barely any laws governing deer hunters. For example, in most other states there are laws against hunting from motorized vehicles to give the animal an even shake, but not in Texas. Texans have expanded on the freedom and built deer stands on top of cars and trucks. Instead of having to walk miles to a cactus stand, Texas hunters just have to fall out of their pickup and climb to an equally comfortable easy chair strapped to the roof.

Texans cruise the deer beds once strapped in, slowing only to take a steadier bead. During the hunting season drive-in restaurants easily handle the two-level food service. Texans build them as high as they want, taking into consideration only low bridge and power line restrictions. During off-season they are used outside drive-in movies, high school football games, and sorority house windows.

✔ *OTHER TYPES OF DEER STANDS:* There are many manufacturers of tree stands designed to provide a comfortable seat, with lightweight alloy metal and in full camo. Several models are like the tall ladders you used to fall off as a kid and look really natural to a deer used to climbing on garage roofs.

Don't forget the manmade stand opportunities, such as power line structures. Buck has seen many deer in places like power line crosscuts near the Jack Daniels distillery. The tall cross beams holding the wires arcing with million-plus amps are fairly comfortable places to sit. Abandoned oil derricks, and isolated radio and relay towers can be effective stands, too.

LATE BREAKING NEWS: In New York City, the first multiple unit deer stand in the northeast corner of Central Park has just gone condo.

METHODS OF GETTING UP INTO YOUR DEER STAND

There are several fast ways to get into your lofty abode:

✔ Use a block and tackle.
✔ Climb metal pegs or hand-hewn crossbars.
✔ Shimmy the tree with climbing gear.

There are many fast ways to get out of your stand:

✔ Jump with your knees flexed and a prayer in your heart.
✔ Fall forward, taking care to first throw your emptied weapon to your hunting partner.
✔ Slide down hugging the tree for dear life, aligning the knot where yours aren't.

EATING IN THE DEER STAND

It is a proven fact that body heat rises through your head and out your hair into the cold air. Wear a good insulated cap like Buck's and use the inner space like an oven, warming and stacking sandwiches on top of your head.

In this protected area, take the sandwiches out of their plastic bags, particularly if you've washed your hair earlier. There won't be enough heat to melt the butter. However, you'll want to be careful not to put too much mayo on the sandwiches as it can spoil under heat. If you decide to heat your entrée on the fire of your loins, leave the bologna sandwiches in the bag for sanitary reasons.

A TYPICAL DAY IN A DEER STAND IN NORTHERN MINNESOTA

ONE HALF HOUR BEFORE SUNRISE—Walk in, climb into stand.

NEXT HOUR—Wait for your overheated body to cool down and soak your clothes.

NEXT HOUR—Prepare to freeze your cajones off.

NEXT HOUR—Eat your first sandwich.

NEXT HOUR—Fantasize about a desperate housewife. The one in the brown house. Married to the accountant.

NEXT HOUR—Wipe nose on sleeve.

NEXT HOUR—Fantasize about high school sweetheart. The one who didn't put out. At least not with you.

NEXT HOUR—Eat second sandwich.

NEXT HOUR—Fantasize about your brother's wife's younger sister.

NEXT HOUR—Go number two. (See section on Big Job.)

NEXT HOUR—Fantasize about another desperate housewife. The one in the brick house. Married to the dentist.

NEXT HOUR—Wipe nose on other sleeve.

NEXT HOUR—Fantasize about and plan strategy on last night's barmaid.

ONE HALF-HOUR BEFORE SUNSET—Climb out of stand, walk out.

P.S. If you start fantasizing about your ex-wife, you can leave the stand early.

DRIVING DEER: The second most popular method of hunting deer is not taking a deer family out for a ride. Deer driving is pushing deer into the firing range of a fellow deer hunter. This method is more physically demanding but most time-effective in the harvest of deer. Some backwater states don't allow the driving of deer, but most civilized game officials encourage this fast-paced sport. There are two roles in driving, the driver and the stander.

The drivers are the more aggressive of the two and have to be restrained on occasion. A driver hangs aluminum pots and pans around his neck and ties a helium balloon to his cap to let the stander both hear and see him. The technique is to dress like a hockey goalie and throw yourself into the deepest and toughest cover big bucks prefer. Drivers yearn to be standers and standers quickly become sitters and then sleepers. As you'd suspect, the most junior in the camp are drivers and try to recruit new drivers during preseason.

HILL HUNTING: Success ratio one hundred percent. The technique is to have hunters surround the hill, banging pots and pans with wooden spoons, forcing the deer to where they want to be anyway, and your pilot pals pop them off for an easy roll down to your pickup. This method is most commonly found in areas with high concentrations of special ops vets.

HUNTING FROM A HORSE: The advantage in hunting from a horse is that a deer will think you are part of the horse, admittedly the ugliest part.

Even though the horse's head seems designed to hold and center a high-powered rifle, Buck does not recommend except in rare occasions using the skull as a bench rest. Buck knows that the thick skull and relative brightness of a saddle horse should qualify it as a hunting prop. Pull your gloves over the bronco's ears before firing and brace yourself for a second recoil.

Horses have long memories and once shot from, should be given to the in-laws as bridle ponies. Other shooting positions include from the side, Indian style, or from under the horse, Hollywood stunt style. The second position, if not done properly, will lessen your horse's stud career aspirations.

If you're hunting alone, let the critter go where it wants. They like to run through deep snow or deep cactus cover where deer hide. If you're hunting with others, tie your bridle to the rear strap of the horse in front.

> **BUCK'S BONUS TIP: All four-legged big animals are kinfolk under that fur and deer will come up to a horse to rub noses and sniff its butt. If this happens, lay tight to the saddle and shoot backwards.**

HUNTING FROM A PIT: In actively hunted areas, it becomes necessary to seek alternatives to deer stands. Deer avoid areas with trees that go BOOM. Mature animals look up, searching for ugly human growths on second growth trees. Many of Buck's cronies take advantage of deer walking around with their eyes to the sky by going underground. All that's needed is a pit deep enough to squat in, a screen thick enough to hold cover, and an active trail to place it in.

Have your partner cover your screen with twigs and dirt and brush the human footprints off the trail, then quietly wait for that trophy buck to use your blind as a scrape.

HUNTING FROM A COMMERCIAL VEHICLE: Riding an Amtrak commuter train from Washington, D.C. to New York one day, a graduate of Buck's Wilderness School became excited and popped off several rounds at a herd of whitetail standing in a New Jersey wasteland and was able to track his animal down several days later.

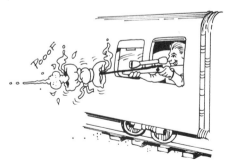

There are complicated laws regarding the discharge of firearms from a public conveyance, such as metro and long distance buses, especially now with homeland security issues. These should be carefully checked before you pack a piece for such a road hunt. Practice common courtesy at all times. In the smaller buses, hunters should only use the window seats or the back row. Shots fired out a back window will be muffled by the loud diesel engines. When you stop to dress the animal, it's traditional to offer the heart or liver to the driver or engineer. By federal law, the baggage compartments under large tour buses have been designed to carry at least six adult deer per compartment.

HUNTING FROM BOATS, CANOES, AND INNER TUBES:

Boats are used both to hunt from and to take you to areas the less fortunate can only dream about. Commercial fishermen in Alaska hunt all year off their poop decks for unsuspecting deer coming down to drink near their illegal gill nets. Large boats are restricted to the more public waters but the smaller cigarette boats can take you right where the larger bucks have their summer cottages. Boats powered by airplane engines are the trickiest to shoot from, since you are traveling much faster than the animal. If you are unable to lead the animal properly, have the captain ram the damn animal. Some states let you hunt from powerboats only on private waters and almost never near public beaches when swimmers are nearby.

Should you catch a fast drift around a bend in a river and run right in the middle of a herd migration, throttle down and throw your anchor rope over the horns of the largest buck. This maneuver is great sport and leads to all sorts of interesting events on shore. Don't shoot an animal in the water. It isn't fair or legal and the hole in the deer will fill with water and sink the deer. Let them reach shore where they will stand for a few minutes while shaking off water, or roll out of your boat on top of them like a Navy SEAL, hog-tie them underwater, and drift with the critter to the nearest sandbar.

Canoes are a traditional native hunting boat. Young braves stand in the bow of the boat, anxious to let their poisoned arrows fly. When they first used rifles, the recoil would knock them back into the boat, punching holes in the birch bark. Not until the invention of fiberglass were they able to hunt like they used to. Some of our finest hunters, like the infamous H. Baxter, the Wyoming Wildman, use canoes to get to the dense cover along river bottoms and those small islands in a river where the more prosperous deer have second homes. Islands and peninsulas are very easy to drive with two people— one pushing the animals to the pointed ends of the landform. Deer should be completely dead (X's in their eyes) before you put them in the canoe to return to camp.

Inner tubes or float tubes with a seat strap are very popular. Build a blind over your tube that looks like a little island. Much to their surprise, several old belly bloaters have had deer swim out to their tube to browse on the foliage. The hunters slipped below and held the deer under until they snorted uncle. White water floating is the highest form of hunting adventure.

HUNTING WITH DOGS: Dogs are used in Canada to track wounded non-resident hunters. In the southeast United States, dogs are used to push deer past pre-positioned stands through cover so thick you can only shoot the smell of a deer. The cover is so thick other hunters can't move about and the canines become your little driving partners. They are not supposed to catch the deer. Their role is to slowly push them by hunters. The dogs are typically mixed breeds and the weapons of choice are shotguns loaded with buckshot. These hunting rites have evolved from coon hunts. Coon dogs are trained to push animals up into trees and, unless the branches are really low, deer find climbing very difficult.

Buck requests that you respect the traditions of dog hunting by using at least a medium-sized dog. There is no reason to add insult to injury by using dachshunds or Chihuahuas. Shorthaired dogs slip through the brush best. Longhaired dogs pick up enough bristle to become camouflaged early in the day, but you'll want to keep these dogs apart at day's end because they will stick together and be difficult to kennel. French Canadians, always at the forefront of forest fashion, use lightly trimmed poodles for tracking, dipping them in camo paint for greater effectiveness.

Bird dogs are used in deer drives but only pointers. Duck dogs are not much good after the first jump from the tree stand.

In the story of Bambi, our hero defended his new bride, Faline, against hunters' dogs and suffered a wound to the shoulder, which just goes to show you—never feed your dogs shoulder cuts. It spoils them.

HUNTING LIKE INDIANS: Early warriors ranked hunting right up there with warfare and, in a wooden fashion, handing out store-bought cigars as manly pursuits. Deer were hunted according to need and most often by large herds of hunters. These warriors wore full natural camouflage, complete with actual heads and hides. Their weapons, according to cultural development, were spears, bows and arrows, snares, and traps. Once they had traded sufficient beaver pelts for epidemics of white man's smallpox and syphilis, they were finally able to lay their hands on firearms.

The most favorite native method of hunting deer was by drives. Most commonly, prairie fires were set to drive deer to water or other ambush sites. Tribes now extinct set their fires upwind of their villages. Fire "surrounds" wrapped a herd of deer with three sides of blaze, with the ambushing party at the mouth of the U. This technique had the advantage of providing precooked venison.

Other types of drive included:

✔ *CHASE TO WATER:* You can't lead a buck to water, but a well-organized drive will certainly make him bob for bullets.

✔ *CHASING OVER CLIFFS:* A technique made famous by old buffalo hunters, deer were run off cliffs producing the first tenderized meat product on the market.

✔ *DRIVING ALONG FENCES INTO ENCLOSURES:* Trees were dropped along a line, which created an ever-shrinking corral, pushing the animals into small pens where warriors waited to take scalp.

According to commercial salmon fishermen, all the above practices are still being used on the major reservations.

DEER LODGES, RACK RANCHES, AND GUIDES

✔ *DEER LODGES:* Buck has long dreamt of a trip to one of these privileged corporate enclaves, where the beds are softer, the meals less greasy, and cognacs and Cuban cigars close each evening. These lodges are constructed from old growth logs, the verticals often still holding a spotted owl nest, with huge stone fireplaces, chandeliers made of old wagon wheels hanging over a dining table covered by linen, decorated with fine silver and china and wildflowers in bud vases, and groaning under a game feast of Olympian proportions. The chef is an accomplished hunter and knows how to capture the essential flavors of the day's hunt. The owner/manager can discuss with equal grace the custom guns of yore or the proper way to skin out a cape. The serving girls all wear pretty outfits cut tight across the bodice, squeezing the little darlings toward their chin. The wines are fine and the conversation enlightening. While you may run into a boor occasionally, the other hunters are people you want to keep in touch with. It's to a place like this that Buck wants to retire.

✔ *RACK RANCHES:* In recent years, hunting-for-profit rack ranches have popped up across the country, offering lazy city-dwellers and other ne'er-do-wells a quick opportunity for a misplaced shot at a trophy mammal. A refinement of these shooting galleries are those stocked with exotics from other lands: elands, giraffes, koala bears, adolescent Mau Mau children, the Lion King, dik diks, and baby elephants.

✔ *GUIDES:* Due to pressure from guide associations, state game officials have slapped guide requirements on many non-residents and their money meters can average $300 to $500 US or $15,000 Canadian a day, depending on the package. To properly check out guides, write the game department in the state you wish to hunt for their approved list, and contact those guides in the area you have selected. Ask them for references and proof they know how to bag deer in the shape of a nice rib roast or several steaks from a recent hunt. This request will show how serious they are and if enough guides respond, you're well on your way to a full freezer. Politely ask for their ages and hunt only with the older guides who'll most likely get tired before you. Master guides are offended by gratuities. The best thanks for a successful trophy hunt are a warm smile and a firm handshake.

SPECIAL METHODS OF HUNTING

SCENTS: Compared to the sensitive instrument of a deer, your nose is a parking lot for boogers. You are naked out there, my friend. You can't smell a deer but they can smell you and much before you come into range.

WHAT YOU SMELL LIKE TO A DEER

You have two choices, both of them good and most effective when combined. First, you must mask your own stink, and second add scents that attract the animals. If you had lutefisk for dinner the night before, the first job is much larger than the second. In scents, you are what you eat and all your vices produce an odor signature. If you have a particularly bad odor problem, cut your underwear out of a large plastic bag so your stink can't escape.

✔ *MASKING SCENTS* are available from perfume factories or from your own making. Commercial scents are easier, but a smell appropriate for Wyoming may not work in Minnesota. The perfume of the nouveau riche wafting through Jackson Hole would curl the nose hairs of a bachelor Norwegian farmer.

It's easy to make your own scent. Scrape dirt that a deer has anointed into a glass jar, filling it halfway. Take it home, add distilled water to the top of the jar, and let sit in a warm room for a couple of days. Filter out the dirt through an old tee shirt and use the remaining fluid as your very own custom scent. You are carrying on in the traditions of the great perfumeries and, if you do this right, you'll have to hoard these fragrances from your hunting party.

✔ *ATTRACTING SCENTS* used by proactive trophy hunters consist of two main types: one that smells like the food they like, or one that attracts bucks displaying their sexual or territorial dominance.

Food lures are hints of what a deer likes to eat: apples, acorns, and corn on the cob. All these aromas can be bought through mail order. It's much easier to squirt on a little liquid lunch than haul in corncobs or steal acorns out of squirrel hidey-holes.

Love scents are best bought commercially, as it is difficult for the average hunter to pinch off the love glands of a live doe. The commercial scents are tenderly squeezed from penned animals that have volunteered for such social experiments. There is no evidence their country cousins can identify city smells from these "kept" animals. The most popular scent is doe urine and used throughout the season to attract bucks curious about their plumbing. Doe-in-heat urine attracts the big horny bucks. Drives their nuts nuts if you know what I mean. Don't spill any of this on your pants if you know what's good for you. Doe urine mixed with food scent appeals to both the prurient interests and food appetite of a buck.

 BUCK'S BONUS TIP: Doe urine mixed with prune juice is effective in attracting older bucks.

Where do you apply these scents? Masking scents should be applied liberally as if getting ready for a date: behind your ears, a little spray on the wrist, a five-day pad under the arm, and behind your knees. If you had a second helping of lutefisk, spray extra in your underwear. Scents last three days, so these masks will linger until you get home. If the scent comes in an atomizer, have a buddy spray it on you. It also doesn't hurt to spray a little on a piece of cloth and attach to the back of your boots, wiping away your foot odor as you walk in. If you ate jalapeño chips the night before, spray a little in your pants before you head out.

If you are trying to attract deer, scent bottles should be set out within range of your weapon. Place on fence posts, tree stumps, or anything off the ground because deer don't like to bend over a lot and the ground winds will help spread the good aromas throughout a target-rich environment.

New products are continually popping up on the market. For example, there are camo tablets you're supposed to take that will neutralize your insides by opening day. The Peace Corps distributes tablets to Third World countries like Germany, where national foodstuffs in intestinal casings create toxic waste problems. A new lubricant and bore cleaner actually masks gun smells but due to the publisher's rush to get this book out, Buck couldn't get in his two scents worth.

RATTLING: During the rut, a buck can be called in by imitating a fight between two bucks, using either real or artificial horns. You can use horns that aren't worth hanging on the trophy wall or buy artificial ones from a taxidermist or sporting goods catalog. A few of the artificial antlers are two right sides to prevent bashing your knuckles, but smart deer can tell the difference—the resulting sound is as odd as two right hands clapping. Pieces of bone in a bag also work well. Just shake the bag for action. Be prepared for the unexpected. If you get good at this, you may have to defend yourself. A big stag has the edge. His huge rack is firmly attached to hundreds of pounds of sweaty sinew while your little plastic horns are hand held and will sound inadequate in a long battle for turf or tush.

BUCK'S BONUS TIP: If you happened to bag an antlerless deer with your bucks-only license, strap your rattling horns on its head and prop the animal up in your window as you drive by the game check station, properly honking the number and types of game taken.

In the sub-sub zero coldest of the winter season, the loose teeth of the largest bucks rattle and old-timers take an extra set of dentures into the woods to rattle up a monster.

DEER CALLS: Many of the new breeds of hunters are adopting an old hunting trick by calling their deer within closer range to be shot. This is done several ways:

✔ *NATURAL CALLS:* Old-timers had to use what Mother Nature gave them and there are just a few left who can make calls with their own mouth. As you'll note, the new calls have no teeth in them and that's because these old guys either had no teeth or had broken dentures. Deer dentures aren't that good either. Just a short "ugh" from the diaphragm level may do it.

✔ *ARTIFICIAL CALLS:* A large cottage industry now services the demand for calls that sound and taste good. Most look like a duck call, are made from fine hardwoods, and a few look somewhat like an autoerotic device and should not be used in mixed company.

✔ *MECHANICAL CALLS:* In some states, you can bring a CD or tape player to your stand, powered either by battery or an extension cord plugged into your car's cigarette lighter. The advantage of these calls is you can turn them up real loud, driving the deer crazy. The tapes and compact discs of these calls are made at game farms under the most unhappy conditions. For example, squeezing penned fawns too hard produces the bleating or distress calls.

The types of calls are:

✔ *THE BLEAT:* Usually done by fawns who are hurt, hungry, lost, or who want to go to the zoo to see their city cousins. When you do this call, bleat like your kids at a toy store. The high-pitched "meows" will break a doe's heart.

✔ *THE SNORT:* A danger call and one you should pay attention to, especially if behind you. The sound is similar to the one made by your mother-in-law when you described your dreams for her daughter.

When deer snort, they are exhaling, forcing nasal wind through a dense forest of twigs and boogers. To mimic them, don't inhale! Blow through the call, aiming it at the deer. Don't spit into the call as someone else might want to use it later.

To snort the natural way, wrinkle your nose, aim nostrils forward and blow real hard, taking care to lean slightly forward so your sinuses don't empty on your new gear.

✔ *THE GRUNT:* A social call with three main uses: to call attention to an occasion, to tend a harem, and to be aggressive in a party situation. It sounds like your brother-in-law at his most intelligible.

Be alert as all three sound like the fourth grunting sound—the grunt that signals that a large animal is moving his bowels. If you accidentally mimic that call, the animals will think it's safe and spend their entire day going toilet. D. "Snorting" Horton of Seattle once flushed out a buck while flushing out his own system and his wild woman, Dot, is still trying to get his clothes clean.

You have an obligation to know the different calls so as not to confuse the animals. For example, it's not appropriate to use a fawn call when surrounded by dry does. Experiment—try pulling in a spike buck with a dying big buck call, created by alternating grunts with heavy wheezing. Once you have mastered the calls, feather the sounds with your hand or hankie to sound more sincere. When you strum the heartstrings of a deer, you will see its ears face forward, its tail a-wagging, and its nose up and sniffing for another furry friend.

Deer like all calls, however. If you are near a lake and forgot your deer call, use your duck call. It'll put the deer's mind to rest as the two like to play together near the lake. It doesn't hurt to put a dying rabbit or squealing squirrel call on the tape deck. Deer are very curious about how small animals die. The sounds are part of a busy, generally happy wood.

A note of caution: If you are really good at calling, you may call in another caller. If caught in this situation, slip quietly away so the other caller doesn't lose face.

ANIMAL MIMICRY: Late breaking technology regarding rattling and scents have brought the proactive hunter ever closer to his quarry. Some of Buck's friends will take the mimicking of animal habits a bit further.

Mock rubs and scrapes have been made possible by the easy availability of scents. During preseason, trophy hunters will take last year's antlers and deer legs into prime habitat and create natural signs, complete with the appropriate smells.

Mock beds are made by sweeping away surface debris from a likely looking spot and lying in the slight depression with your buckskins on. Deer drool while sleeping, so the research and development folks at the scent manufacturers are perfecting drool for the drooling marketplace.

Mock droppings are also available for a hunter's tool kit. Collected by feedbags attached to zoo animals, these marbles come with a juice to complete the gift package. Serious hunters will warm these pellets between their cheeks before placing them on a buck run.

Mock animals are the ultimate mimicry devices. Buy a two-piece deer suit down at the local costume shop, use the latest scents made of dehydrated tarsal glands and droppings, and start your doe love calls. If it works, you'll want to be in the front half of the costume.

STAYING DOWNWIND: A forest of pulp has been spent telling you to stay downwind of deer to score. Do you realize how hard that is? Are those writers nuts? Some even suggest you build four stands—one for each wind direction—east, west, north, and south! What if the wind shifts to the northwest? Next season they'll recommend eight stands and double their consulting fees from the tree stand manufacturers. If you listened to all these armchairs, you'd spend the entire summer building stands. Buck is also expecting to see recommendations on heights of deer stands according to daily thermal changes. Never mind. Build your tree stand like Buck's—wrap it around the tree so if the wind shifts, so can you.

UNUSUAL METHODS OF HUNTING

Each state loses a good percentage of their critters by methods not regularly listed. For example, West Virginia harvested 240,000 total deer in one year and of these, almost 11,000 were taken "non-seasonally." You can probably learn from these alternative style harvests. Here is the breakdown.

✔ *AUTOMOBILES:* Detroit engineers have always added more weight in the front bumpers to help you harvest a steak off the highway. Your mechanical monster is an acceptable way to dispatch a doe to deer heaven. Aim to hit only the less tasty parts and hold really tight to the steering wheel. If you are on a busy street, don't field dress the animal there. Throw it into your trunk and do the work at home. Some states require you let someone know, but it's not clear which states these are or who to call. Some states are experimenting with reflectors that flash like deer eyes to put more animals near the centerline. In many western states this source of fresh meat has been the exclusive property of game warden and highway cop families, so be careful or quick.

✔ *CROP DAMAGE:* In agricultural states, if deer are eating your market goods, whether plantation crops, apple trees, or cannabis, you can take those hungry rascals at leisure. It doesn't matter if you own the property, all you have to do is occupy it and be able to prove to a game warden that crop damage has been done. If the damage isn't noticeable, get a couple of friends on tractors to trash the area like a herd of deer would.

BUCK'S BONUS TIP: In many areas, hard to tell where, it's illegal to hunt deer over piles of cracked corn, even though it's your cracked corn. (For you city folk, cracked corn is not on the cob.) You aren't supposed to use apples either, unless they can't be used for baking. Some property owners plant tasty forage only for deer, but it's better to use crops genetically engineered to encourage maximum bone growth. Clinically similar to drugs used to encourage maximum human male bone growth, these start working within an hour. If a buck has maximum growth that lasts more than four hours, call the vet.

✔ *ILLEGAL:* Poaching is a year-round activity in most states and a spectator sport in most of the Deep South. Game meat from all sources is a low-cost reception food for redneck weddings. The backstrap is traditionally reserved for and enjoyed by the headtable. With the possible exception of the bride in a "delicate" condition. The chops are reserved for the wedding party. Guests and their parole officers are feted with an offally tasty stew made of spare parts.

✔ *DOGS:* Near large metropolitan areas, huge bands of undersized pets frustrated at being so small and ugly will chase deer for two weeks hoping to knock one down, and take another month to eat it.

✔ *FENCES:* It's not known exactly how to hunt with fences. Buck assumes the weapon are those automatic fence gates with heavy metal doors that catch and squeeze deer to death as they try to get to greener pastures. Introducing remote control closures have allowed fence hunters to do well in recent years.

✔ *TRAINS:* In northern states this is a much larger problem, especially as snow forces deer to higher ground. The cowcatchers on the large freight trains damage the meat and the engineers will not stop the train for small run-ins. If there is a large bump, the conductor will stop the train so that tourists can take pictures.

METHODS OF THE HUNTED

Experienced animals have their wisdom and ingenuity to thank for keeping their headgear. After opening day, deer lose their happy innocence and will not stand still to be petted. All the horrors of the last season are remembered and they try all the tested ways to avoid meeting their maker.

CIRCLING BACK: Hunted deer will quietly circle back around the unwary hunter and come up close enough to sniff the hunter's butt. If you feel a wet nose, turn slowly so as not the scare the animal.

Young animals like party games, especially Peek and Bleat. They simply must know who the new creature is.

HOLDING TIGHT: Many a savvy animal will lie still in good cover when a hunter walks by. Many hunters, especially those raised on Disney reruns, look only for standing animals.

There have been reports of trophy animals that have "held tight" so long that they cannot walk and have to be tended by other deer friends who bring water and regurgitated acorns.

Sometimes a mule deer will stand tight, thinking that you are expecting a moving animal but that never works since they can't hold their breath that long.

When pushed, big animals jump blindly into deep cover, thinking no hunter will follow. The evidence is loud crashing ahead of you and if you listen close enough, you'll hear the grunts and groans of the animal hitting trees and hidden stumps. Smart deer don't bolt into tall timber—it hurts too much. If you hear this commotion, follow the animal tracks up to the edge and peer into the darkness. You'll likely see a busted-up animal that needs to be put out of his misery. The broken trophy rack can be made into buttons.

If cornered, a large deer will rush a hunter, and most state laws allow shooting in self-defense if you can prove you warned the animal first.

WEAPONRY

RIFLES: There are long and short rifles. Short rifles have louder booms, longer rifles shoot further and straighter. Every deer book carries an opinion on what rifle to carry, so Buck is going to give you a little history and only one opinion and two maxims.

You really should carry a weapon that becomes you. If you are tall and lanky, carry a long lean piece. If you are short and stocky, stay home.

Buck's two favorites are:

✔ *THE 30-30 MODEL 94:* There were only 30 of these 30 caliber guns made in 1930 by a gunsmith named Wn. (short for Winfred) Chester who in his mid thirties was considered an up and coming gunsmith. This gun is fun to shoot, especially in the brush, and can be carried in good-looking leather holsters called scabbards that are traditionally tied to horses but can also be attached to motorbikes, ATVs, or a new wife.

✔ *THE 30-06:* A much larger gun with a longer barrel. The ammo is very easy to find. Even the churches in small hunting towns carry it if you drop enough loose change in the collection basket. Buck carries it in bolt action as he kills with only one shot and is getting close to averaging less than one bullet per animal. He will fire a second shot only if there is another animal hiding behind the first and will use the same hole.

Buck prefers these guns mostly because they were given to him!

✔ *MAXIMUM MAXIM:* The best rifle for you is the one you can best shoot deer with.

✔ *MAXIMUM MAXIM 2:* If your best rifle looks like a rag-tag pass-me-down, like Buck's old Springfield, leave it in the case while staying at a well-heeled game lodge. Buck takes a very expensive loaner from a gun shop to display while signing in at the lodge and then sneaks out his old killer stick once the hosts are back inside drinking cognac.

SCOPES AND SIGHTS: Scopes are for people whose eyes, like their other body parts, are no longer what they used to be. They are single glass binoculars fitted on top of your weapon. The insides vary with different kinds of what's called reticules but all are expensive adaptations of crosshairs.

Some hunters will paste a drawing of a deer on the front lens and, when a real animal fills the outline, simply pull the trigger. If you like to shoot at greater distances just for the sport of it, mount your scope on backwards.

✔ *IRON SIGHTS:* These come as standard equipment on new guns and a gun shouldn't be considered a true gift unless there are scope mounts attached and another box under the Christmas tree.

✔ *PEEP SIGHTS:* Standard equipment on military weapons. For the ex-military types who buy these relics, peeping is a way of life. Peep sights are commonly mistaken for "peek" sights, which are any optical device used to peek in the bedroom/bathroom window of a desperate housewife.

BULLETS: Factory loads do not refer to the blue-collar union workmen that made them but to store-bought shells, which are the safest to shoot. They are made under the tightest controls and are test fired under laboratory conditions at animals illegally purchased from unscrupulous zoo managers.

There is an entire industry built around the reloading of your own shells. You can buy bullets, gunpowder, and shells from catalogs and custom build your own guided missiles in the safety of your basement. For the sake of your neighbors, reload your shells in a concrete basement and, if you are ordering gunpowder, ask that it be shipped first class for all the special handling the post office is known to deliver. Test fire your custom loads away from other people and tell your wife where you will be shooting should you be late for dinner. And breakfast the next morning.

Whether you're using your own reload or a factory bullet, you want a bullet that slowly expands in the first deer, mushrooming to mid-size in the second, and exploding in the third. The oomph behind the bullet is the gunpowder and the trick is to cram as much powder in as the cartridge can stand without blowing up. Your hunting buddies are always willing to try your custom loads so you don't have to ask them. Just put a few in their gun belt. They'll let you know how they liked them.

The oomph will peter out if the deer is a long ways off. The path of the bullet is called the "ejaculatory." The ejaculatory describes the rise and fall of the bullet from the time it's fired to the time it lands on the animal. This information is important as you gauge your shots. If the animal is too close, you may have to back up quite a ways to make a proper hit.

MUZZLELOADERS: If you like to wear buckskins and put grass in your moccasins, your weapon of choice will be a "smokepipe." These guns are loaded from the wrong end and have a bore that's as big as the one carrying it. There are small-bore boors, too. Except for those who wear coonskin caps while watching Davy Crockett reruns on the Disney Channel, most real hunters are puzzled by the enthusiasm for these popguns. It's estimated there are more black powder hunters now than back when they should have been. You have a choice of using a flintlock, which is more authentic but outlawed, or a percussion weapon. The original weapons are too dangerous and expensive to shoot so replicas are the common choice among these replica hunters.

The only thing muzzleloaders remember after a shot is a great cloud of smoke. By the time the mushroom cloud disappears, the deer, which was out of the short range of this goofy weapon, will be in the next county. You can pick out a muzzleloader in a crowd by the surprised expression on his face and, more importantly, the powder burns around his eyes and nose.

Things to do while you're waiting for the smoke to clear:

Go home and mow the lawn.
Have friends over for lunch.
Sleep.

Due to the short ejaculatory of a muzzleloader, most of these Kit Carsons shoot their deer lying down, often in their own bed.

There are several advantages to hunting with a blunderbuss. Game wardens think you odd enough to schedule a separate season. The needed wadding materials will rid you of old tee shirts. Novice shooters shoot their wad too early. You get to use your purse for the precious little accessories. Best of all, it's easy to find your deer, coughing their way into the swamp.

Muzzleloaders require perfect weather so the powder in the pan won't blow away. A flash in the pan best describes the social and hunting skills of these hunting romantics. Latecomers to the sport are now customizing their muzzleloaders with scopes. Some even use new in-line muzzleloaders once their fellow buck skinners are inside their tepees. Others will slip a modern handgun into the large caliber breech when the Kit Carson du jour isn't looking. They strive for authentic gear by using deerskin to cover a thermos bottle and hand-sewing buckskin over their goose down trousers.

The only verified cases of deer laughing are reported by old-timers who have watched the animals peek above ridges overlooking muzzleloaders in make-believe rendezvous. Gnarled old bucks tell the young ones giggling at the camps that's the way it used to be.

Muzzleloading is seen by respected sociologists as an attempt to regain our more innocent past. When early settlers had a chance to use modern weapons, they threw their old muzzleloaders away.

SHOTGUNS: Shotgun hunting is required by law where game wardens have determined there are too many hunters hunting too close together or they want to keep the more sophisticated rifles from a local population who talk in single-syllable words.

A twelve-gauge shotgun is the most effective size and many states will set minimums for you. The range is typically one hundred yards or less. Double-barrel shotguns give you twice the chance to miss an animal. Since slugs are the most commonly used ammunition, buy a specially barreled slug gun and shoot slugs only. If you shoot slugs through your regular shotgun barrel, you'll have a wider choke for duck hunting later in the year.

00- and 0-size shot follow in popularity. If you plan to use buckshot, you must shoot close enough. To gauge the range, take your wife's buckskin coat, hang it on a clothesline, and fire a few rounds. The charge will blow off a few buttons, but when you think that the coat is normally full of muscle and flank steaks, you'll understand what Buck is telling you.

In several states you can carry over/under guns, a shotgun barrel mounted under a rifle barrel. With this oddity you can walk the legal boundary between the two weapons and fire in either direction.

The real danger in the use of shotguns is lead poisoning. So many deer are hit but not killed by shotguns that tens, maybe millions of deer go to the

Big Swamp, dying a terrible death. After three shotgun hunters from Wisconsin hit an adult deer, the poor beast was carrying enough lead to show up on radar. Constipation, fatigue, and abdominal cramps quickly followed.

PISTOLS AND HANDGUNS: What with all the rifles that don't have a good home, there is really no need to hunt with a pistol. Action movies with shorthaired heroes sporting aviator glasses have created a mob of Pistol Petes who have taken to the field. Thoughtful writers have nicknamed pistols "handguns" for the slower shooters who are not sure which appendage to hold them with.

Check with your local legals for permission to hunt with your Dirty Harry Special. Criminal law, not hunting regulations, governs handgun use and with over 20,000 laws in the U.S. governing the ownership and use of pistols, you have a lot of reading to do before you take to the woods.

When buying a pistol, order special barrel extensions from custom gunsmith. The longer the barrel, the better the shot. Buck prefers a barrel at least thirty-six inches long.

Most handguns have an effective range of up to fifty yards. Hold the gun steady with both hands, or lean the barrel on a hard surface, like your mother-in-law's head. If your hands are shaky from losing a fight with Black Jack, you'll need all the help you can get.

Pistols work best in deepest cover, and the hunter should have at least two properly holstered. Deer aren't bright enough to move faster than your quick draw and if they are city deer, they will appreciate a look at how the West was won.

BOWHUNTING: Bowhunters look at rifle shooters like fly fishermen look at bass anglers. Archers think themselves the purists, the practitioners of the quiet art. With a dismal success rate, they say they hunt more for sport than meat, yet have a wider support network for consolation and extended therapy.

Bowhunters work under all sorts of disadvantages. The limited overall success rate is not strong enough to convince your old lady you are really hunting while away from home. How does she know you're not just screwing around with your pals, coming home empty-handed with liquor on your breath and stinking from days of intense male bonding? How can you justify all the new gear? Game wardens give you a break with an earlier season, usually during warm fall days and in some states, if you missed making a four-legged pincushion, you can still bag a buck with a rifle. The warden is under oath not to tell your fine furred friends.

To successfully bowhunt, you must get closer to deer or have them snuggle up closer to you. Your own stink must be masked with stronger smells that are familiar to deer. In farm country, rub fresh manure all over your body. In deep woods, cover yourself with freshly squeezed skunk cologne.

Sound moves faster than your arrow. The "twang" may reach the ears of the animal before your broadhead hits their broad head. The final ignominy is when the deer absolutely ignores not only your presence and presents but tail-flips a BA on the way out of range.

Traditional long bows are being replaced by very sophisticated compound bows with pulleys, stabilizers, and scopes. The pulleys are designed to make it easier for these traditionally weaker hunters. Several manufacturers have given their latest hi-tech bows to local native chiefs who are still on page one of the instruction booklet. Another outfit is trying to build an over/under bow, with a high-powered rifle as a stabilizer, which will create a hole for the arrow to go in.

Like muzzleloaders, bowhunters must be aware of the urge to adopt the authentic weapons of their Cro-Magnon relatives. Flint is harder to find now and bows made out of saplings are splinter factories. It's difficult to buy the proper poisons, too.

TRAPS, SNARES, AND NETS: These methods are not quite legal and certainly not nice but they were perfected by white market hunters and used in cultural backwaters with great success.

Netting is by far the most popular, due to its relatively low cost. An Alaskan native can string a gill net between two trees and, placing a salt lick on the far side, snag those deer looking for more seasoning in their bland diet.

EQUIPMENT

Buck doesn't recommend any manufacturers and that's why this book is so skinny. Sportswear and equipment companies back their semi-trailers up to the homes of outdoor magazine publishers to gain a few favored words but Buck, while a bit underdressed, gives you the real skinny.

The best equipment you can get is your Dad's. The gear is free and field-tested.

The next best set is whatever you can assemble out in the garage. Older brothers always leave gear behind, especially if they marry a city girl. Whatever you are missing, borrow from friends. Cultivate and keep friends with good gear. These people are always buying the latest stuff and will often forget what they loaned you. In fact, once you have borrowed gear, dye the material and stencil your name on. They'll never miss it.

The next best bet is to get down to the local Sears store for farm clothes. Don't go to one of the new look stores where the Arnold Palmer polyester slacks are pushing out the work clothes. Go to an old one where they may still have Ted Williams approved sports attire. Old Ted knew his stuff, as did J.C. Penney, and their brand names like Big Mac, Sears Best, and Carhartt are what separates the residents from the loud, overdressed dudes taking your favor counter seats at the Tic-Toc Cafe. This sturdy wear, once seasoned properly, makes the best pass-me-downs.

It is confusing to buy clothing and gear now. There are too many fabrics, colors, and sizes and all designed to make you dependent on other people's opinions, slipping into the odious realm of fashion. You have to guard against becoming an equipment maven. Buck had to ask one of the camo gun bearers behind the counter in a famous sporting goods shop as to the proper shade of orange for deer hunting. The lesson here is to wear what you like. You can hunt in your street clothes. In Wisconsin, you can hunt in your wife's street clothes, for all it matters. Many do.

The main thing is to be comfortable. If it's cold out, stay warm and vice versa. In Minnesota, the nine-month winters are cold and the first thing to freeze are your fingers, your toes (if stand hunting), and then your rest of body. If your kidneys chill down, prepare to die in the woods.

Buck likes wool: wool jackets, pants, outer socks, caps, and long johns. Buck hunted in wool before it was pre-shrunk, when a wet stocking cap would bring on severe migraine headaches. He'll slip on a cotton sock only if it has been dyed to look like wool. Buy thermal underwear like you buy a sleeping bag, in temperature degree ranges. The best thing to do is ask your mailman or a cop what kind of underwear they wear in the wintertime. Ask them in a deep, serious voice. Some camp girls will wear silk underwear, but be careful around them. In warm weather hunting, all this wool might give you prickly heat, so layer your clothing, taking items off as you warm up and dropping them along the trail to pick up on the way back to the truck. Trails of abandoned gear are a good way to determine how hard hunted an area is and, who knows, you might find something that fits.

Headgear is very important in cold climates since your body heat rises and a good cap will keep it in. Hair also helps, so start letting your hair grow out two to three months prior to season. If you wear a toupee, cut a skullcap from one of your old hides out in the garage. Hairdressers in central Wisconsin are having a banner year in blaze orange toupees. If you are bald or balding, have a loved one put one or two coats of hard wax on your dome to help hold in the heat.

Footwear depends on the method of hunting. If you are tree standing in Minnesota, you need Air Force bunny boots. That need is as good a reason as any to encourage your younger brother to join the armed forces. Give him your shoe size as you see him off at the train station. If you are stalking, wear a boot that's quiet and comfortable, breaking them in at least a day before the season begins.

Good gloves for cold weather are hard to find. Buck has read all the claims, but ten hours in a deer stand in subzero weather will chill out any glove and what's more important here is the ability to slip your hands out of the gloves and down into your pants to catch a little body heat. An old trick to determine outside temperature is to see how far your nuggets have disappeared up into the old bag.

✔ *WHAT TO DO FOR YOUR EYES:* If you wear glasses, bring along another set in case of breakage. Metal-framed glasses are cold in the winter. In high heat, opera glasses, while pretentious, are acceptable, especially in the hunting lodge in the Northeast.

✔ *WHAT TO DO FOR YOUR EARS:* If the loud noise of a gun scares you, you can buy electronic mufflers that amplify natural sounds yet cut out loud ones. If your eyes are really good, you may not need sound at all. Do you hear me on this?

✔ *WHAT TO DO FOR YOUR NOSE:* An electronic nostril expander and odor enhancer has hit the Wisconsin market so hunters can smell the kielbasa back on the camp grill. The nose will automatically shut off when pointing towards another hunter's Big Job.

Okay, you are probably wondering what Buck wears to his Minnesota deer stand:

- ✔ Blaze orange watch cap to keep his sandwiches warm and meet minimum fashion requirements.
- ✔ Hand-me-down faded red wool jacket with a back game bag that leaks and no-name red and black plaid wool trousers that suffer from major fiber breakdown.
- ✔ Blaze orange Gore-Tex gloves that easily hold the outside freezing temperatures inside.
- ✔ Motley assortment of hand-me-down wool socks and two full sets of wool union suits nobody wants to borrow.

CAMOUFLAGE GEAR: Early hunters tried to hide behind trees and under bushes so deer would not recognize them. When the technique wore thin, they covered themselves with natural skins and heads. Military forces picked up on this childlike need to hide out and started big wars to test camouflage gear, which is now available for field sports.

What you look like to a deer:

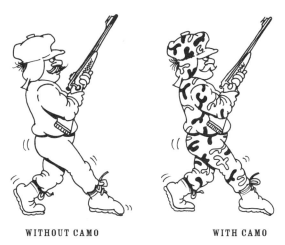

WITHOUT CAMO   WITH CAMO

High fashion has slithered into hunting clothes and camo patterns are now available for most hunting habitats. Expensive trademarks protect the different types and only the most secure hunters dare mix patterns. The key is to select the pattern of your hunting area. The very best is a pattern called "mammoflauge" which features shapes of the two very good reasons why you had to get married.

Fashion designers along Seventh Avenue in Deer Creek, Minnesota are burning the midnight mink oil to bring you a new pattern called Resident Camo, featuring stone washed, mismatched gear in odd, non-fitting sizes.

✔ *PROBLEMS WITH CAMO:* If you lay down in full camo for a snooze, stay away from the trail so another hunter won't sit on you to eat lunch.

It's easy to misplace your camo toilet paper. Worse yet, it's easier to misplace used camo toilet paper.

It's difficult to see other camouflaged hunters, which could lead to all kinds of archery accidents if archers could hit anything.

Camophiles even buy makeup, waxes, paints, and dusts to apply on their skins. Continual practice of these feminine habits has sent quite a few turkey hunters to Denmark for sex changes. Camophiles paint their butt knowing that once your pants are pulled down to take a dump, your cheeks look too much like a butt of a buck to the non-resident hunter on the far ridge.

 BUCK'S BONUS TIP: **Older, more conservative deer tend to see life in black and white terms so camo for these senior bucks is less important.**

DEER HUNTING CHECKLIST

FIREARM

Big Gun

Bullets (lots)

Ear plugs

Recoil pads

Ben Gay

Condoms

ARCHERY

Bow

Arrows

Condoms

Quive

Tricorn Hat

Moccasins

MUZZLELOADER

Balls

Diaphram

HUNTING GEAR

License (optional in
some areas)

Knife

Map

Condomset

Rope

Survival Kit

Radio

Weber grill

Scent

Wrist compass

Chain saw

PERSONAL GEAR

Footwear

Socks

Pants

Shirts

Jacket

Gloves

Cap, hat

Liquor

Custom cue stick

Toilet paper

French tickelers

Beer bottle opener

Camping gear is whatever you took to your Boy Scout cookouts: Tent, sleeping bag, shovel, camp stove, "roofies", condoms, smokes, and ice chest.

WOODSMANSHIP

It is the mark of an experienced hunter to feel comfortable in the woods, with himself and the terrible deeds of blood sport. Comfort comes from knowledge of what's right and wrong, and experience gleaned from many previous seasons. Buck encourages you to mimic the senior members in your camp. Remember that you are on a vacation from a controlled and stressful environment. Relax. Enjoy. While personal hygiene may be of paramount concern to your urban family, in the woods it's a distinct disadvantage to smell like them.

Buck has gathered a short course of tips to help you in all situations. The tips include toilet instructions, what to do when you get lost, and much more. He wraps up with a few calm words about buck fever. Many readers have written Buck about this woodsmanship chapter and said his advice has helped them at home and work, especially the hints about going grunt.

TOILET TIPS: One of the major difficulties of a deer hunt is how to organize trips to the toilet. The very thought of it frightens many a good woman hunter or camp spouse. What's most important is to know your body well and pace food consumption with your daily activity.

For example, if you eat a big breakfast before hunting, use as little grease as possible so the food will hang in better until you have a more convenient time and place to toilet. If you do insist on larding up, eat as soon as you wake and once finished, hop around the cabin to pack that food closer to the exit. Ten minutes before you plan getting into the car for the drive to the stand, walk around the camp, bending over often, trying to squeeze your intestines so they will work in the nearby warm camp setting. If you are a senior member of the camp, the others will wait for you.

The next critical juncture is the walk from the car to the stand in the woods. Quite often, a bumpy ride in will start the desired chain reaction. Before entering the woods, look for a spot to deposit your used groceries.

If you are in a large parking area, a very convenient spot is under the driver's side of the sportsman who built his stand too close to yours. Cover your tracks with camo paper so it will be more of a surprise.

Without fail, the walk to the stand or the first mile of stalking will get results. Set your mind at ease. What you must understand is that the woods in which you hunt is really nothing but a big toilet. Why do you think they keep asking the question about where the bears go? The woods are a toilet for Cock Robin, porcupines, little mice, Mr. Owl, ground squirrels, Thumper, wild turkeys, and, in the exotic game preserve and artillery range, Dumbo. Express your natural urges.

GOING NUMBER 1: Several dos and don'ts for watering the lilies.

1. ***Do not aim upwind*** without wearing water-repellent clothing.
2. ***Do not aim uphill*** without wearing rubber boots.
3. ***Do not aim at trees or bushes.*** These antics identify you as a competing buck in the eternal battle for territories and harems. (See section on forced entry.)
4. ***Do not aim near your stand or deer trail.*** To a clean-living buck, you already smell like a barge of New Jersey garbage and there is no scents in adding to the stink. Wander over and water the stand of that bozo who foiled a good shot last year. If you can hold it, climb up into the stand and whiz all over his lofty abode. Do this when he's not in the stand.

Empty your plastic sandwich bags and fill for later disposal if you are in a stand and don't want to or can't leave. Other containers that work are hot water bottles, heavy-duty garbage bags, oil cans with spouts, and, in emergencies, a thermos. Make sure this one is different from the one with the beef bouillon.

Take your time and enjoy the break from a stressful hunt if you must go wee-wee. After all, it's taken quite a bit of time to find the little fellow who's tried to hide behind layers of long johns, especially those union suits put on backwards. Once you are finished, don't be in such a rush to put that rascal back. Several very famous sportsmen have told Buck that one of their greatest pleasures in the wood is to aim that 30-30 in all directions, hip-shooting at that elusive trophy buck. Nobody is watching.

GOING NUMBER 2: Big Jobs are major efforts, best done in camp or where you park your car. To be absolutely sure a bowel movement is in order, squeeze off a little gas to tell you how close you are to dropping the A-bomb. Several important observations:

1. ***It'll seem like you'll never make it*** to where you want to go.
2. ***You don't know how much clothing you have on*** until you try to take the bottom half down in a hurry.
3. ***You don't know really how cold it is*** until the north wind catches your southern exposure.
4. ***You won't ever know how silly you look.***
5. ***It is very clumsy to shoot from that position.***

Some other very important considerations:

1. ***Squat properly at a correct angle*** so you don't use your pants as toilet paper. Buck shows you how this is best done below:

2. ***Hold onto a small tree*** if an uncontrollable explosion is in the works.

3. ***Carry on and get the job done.*** The only remaining concern is whether you brought toilet paper. A wad stuffed in a back pocket several seasons ago won't do you much good now. A roll a few days old may work. A fresh roll is the sign of a happy hunter, especially one in an official color like blaze orange. If you don't have paper, your only choices are what Mother Nature provides or what you are wearing. In the case of the former, dry maple leaves work fairly well but Mom doesn't provide much help in sagebrush country. Many new hunters will use these commonly found leaves:

POISON OAK

POISON IVY

The worst case scenario involves the sacrifice of a glove, a handkerchief, or a pair of shorts.

BLOWING YOUR NOSE: Often during the most active times of the day, you will have an incredible itching inside your nose, way up there where you can't get a finger, even with your gloves off. Deer don't sneeze like humans so no matter what you do, try to muffle the sneeze. You will not just sneeze once. You will sneeze at least three times.

✔ *OPTION 1.* Take off your cap and, pulling the edges tight around your nose and mouth, sneeze forcefully. This method will force you to eat the sandwiches going cold on top of your head.

✔ *OPTION 2.* Pinch your nose real hard, leaving just a little passageway and inhale fast, trying to pull that ticklish booger way up above the sneeze line. This hardly ever works, especially on opening day.

✔ *OPTION 3.* If you are an experienced and happy hunter, you would have brought a handkerchief. Cup it in your hands and take the attack as best you can.

✔ *OPTION 4.* If you are new to all this and have less than average personal hygiene, pull your long john shirt up over your nose and let the thunderstorm run its wet course.

While cleaning up after a good sneeze, you'll understand why old hunters wear wool jackets.

Preventative measures can help avoid sneezes. If you are on a stand and you sense something going on up there, put one finger tight over the free nostril and blow hard, launching a mucous missile at the ground squirrel playing below.

SMOKING WHILE HUNTING: When smoking cigarettes, keep deer from smelling the noxious, burning weed by walking fast while you exhale so the smoke molecules will scatter. Throw butts only near a competitor's stand or break down the butt, tucking filters into a pant cuffs for later disposal.

All the denizens of the woods enjoy pipes stuffed with an aromatic tobacco. As for cigars, the dime store varieties with artificial fillers are unpopular among non-smoking animals. Cigars made from the original Cuban seeded plants are associated in the deer's mind with hunting lodges and the finer things of shooting sports.

Smoking local hallucinogens enhances an outdoor spiritual experience but will impart anthropomorphic characteristics to the quarry and therefore are best avoided.

SLEEPING DURING THE HUNT: You've been up all night drinking and lying with your pals, or slept uneasily knowing that the camp girl would goose you after you dropped off, and are too tired to hunt all day. The early morning sun is sliding up over the horizon, warming you and your heavy, greasy breakfast and you want to nod off awhile.

First, who cares? Your odds of seeing, much less shooting at, much less actually hitting a deer are so low it won't make any real difference.

Second, who'll know? If you don't make the mistake of walking back to the car and snoozing in the back seat, nobody will have a clue. Don't be obvious by sleeping along a road, trail, or logging path. Turn your face into the leaves if you plan on snoring. Here are some places to sleep:

✔ *ALONG A DEER TRAIL:* If you are a light sleeper, you won't miss a chance to bag an animal here. The smart bucks will let you sleep but then again, odds are you wouldn't have seen them anyway.

✔ *ON A DEER STAND:* Tie yourself to the tree or stand so you don't fall out. Keep the rope tied below your neck.

✔ *ON A DRIVE:* This is possible only if you are a stander. Don't worry about a little catnap—the noise of either a deer or the drivers will wake you in time to blast away.

 ***BUCK'S BONUS TIP:* Oldtimers like to curl up in a recently vacated, still warm deer bed to snooze while the animals are out feeding their faces.**

BUCK FEVER: This is a clinical condition characterized by acute twitching, drooling, glassy eyes, and general disorientation. Similar to shock, the blood pressure is lowered and the affected hunter is pale, with moist, cool skin, nausea, a bit of chest pain, and a rapid pulse rate.

When a large trophy buck enters an unsuspecting hunter's view, his bodily fluids change direction and produce this critical but treatable condition. The spooked hunter will often either freeze up in a mild form of catatonia or enter into hyperactivity, pointing and ejecting shells through his weapon without pulling the trigger.

The only proven treatment is to have the big buck leave the area. If the hunter was on a deer stand when the critter came through, you should look for him in the nearby bushes. Look for any broken bones or spirit. Occasionally there will be spotting in the hunter's underwear and this very human failure should be treated with good humor.

TIPS ON HOW TO AVOID BUCK FEVER

PRESEASON
✔ Practice deep breathing exercises.
✔ Have your third eye checked for glaucoma.
✔ Meet with others with similar affliction in a supportive adult beverage environment.

IN THE DEER STAND
✔ Continue deep breathing exercises.
✔ Quietly apologize to all you have wronged in your adult life.
✔ When you hear a big buck crashing your way through the deep brush, be pre-emptive and take a dump in your pants before he gets into range.

HOW TO ENTER THE WOODS: Most hunters will only go a hundred yards or so into the woods when they hunt. This distance can be like a football field full of nasty surprises if you are not familiar with the terrain. Be brave. Wear a happy face. Wave cheerfully to your hunting buddies even though you are consumed with stark, bone-crushing terror. There are two useful ways to enter the woods.

✔ *BY COMPASS:* Put your back to the tree closest to your parking spot, face the scary woods and take a reading straight into that darkness and start walking in, one foot behind the other like you did in your sobriety test for the highway patrol. Count the number of steps and at each giant step interval, yell out 100, 200, and 300 to set your memory. When you want to leave the woods, reverse the directions by turning the compass upside down and follow the arrow out, walking like you entered, in the same footsteps, looking over your shoulder occasionally so you don't bump into any other armed, psychotic loners.

BUCK'S BONUS TIP: City dweller distance doesn't compute in the north woods. For example, a "block" in a target-rich environment is made of salt. A deer stand is not "one story high," nor "thirty hands high" unless you are a real big horse or super-buck. There is no uptown, cross-town, or downtown. However, there is an up and down, which should be comforting to those who are lost.

✔ *BY TRACKS:* As you go into the woods, mark a noticeable path by breaking small branches and trees, carving tree trunks as you stumble along, or sprinkle corn chips, soap flakes, or bird seed as a visible trail to follow out. This path will also help your friends find you if you get buck fever. Non-residents should tie strings to the car door handles and unroll the ball as they walk in.

GETTING LOST: What do you mean, you're lost? Did Kit Carson or Davy Crockett ever get lost? You bet! They were lost all the time. History books can't account for over half of their days, so you know they were in some godforsaken spot, in a cold sweat panic, and never knowing where their next meal or arrow was coming from. Songwriters couldn't string together the right words to describe their constant state of panic, but if you get lost and admit it, your pals will think you are a goofball and never invite you back. Ways to avoid getting lost:

1. **Don't go in.**
2. **Be the last to go into the woods.** After you are sure everybody is in, go back to the car and snooze out the day. One half hour before dusk, walk backwards into the woods and after fifty feet or so, start strolling out singing happy hunter, Ted Nugent songs.
3. **Never lose sight of a hunting buddy** who knows his way and stay out of his sight all day, snoozing if possible and follow him in the evening, catching up at the road and saying, "This sure was some sort of day, huh? See anything?"
4. **If stalking an area, tie a rope to a tree** in the middle of a clearing and circle hunt as you would ride a crop wheel irrigator.
5. **If you forgot your compass,** point the big hand of your watch toward the sun. Half the distance between the big hand and noon is either true north or south. If you are wearing a digital watch, point the crystal towards the sun and divide the second number by the minutes and that number will face you due south. Except for leap years, remember the sun will always rise in the east and set in California. For those of you not familiar with California, consider yourself fortunate.
6. **If you are really lost**, break the monotony of the woods and show real panic with primal screams, whistling, or shooting off a couple rounds at specified intervals. One shot means one shot or one less Scandinavian at the dinner table. Two shots mean double that. Three shots mean you gut shot the deer or are lost, and either way a loser. Never mind.
7. **Prepare to die.** Dignity in these final moments that seem like days is important to you as a man. Your family would not expect less and your vision of the Great White Whitetail will sustain you.

HUNTING ETHICS

IF ANOTHER HUNTING PARTY IS CROWDING YOUR HABITAT:

Check out their tree stands a few days before the season, making sure they are loosely attached, and/or bird hunt the area with dogs a few days before.

IF SOMEONE ELSE IS IN YOUR STAND: Walk quietly near the stand and crank up the old chain saw. Typically the lost non-resident will vacate your stand or their bowels for you.

If there is a Mexican standoff and you don't feel like Pancho Villa, leave the area and wish the intruder a happy day. Crank up the old chainsaw when you find his vehicle.

If that doesn't do it, declare the stand lost and sprinkle large amounts of deer repellent around the area later.

And for good measure, call the local chapter of Homeland Security and give the official on duty the vehicle license plate, a description of the bomb-making material in the back seat, and the individual himself. Hang on to your hat. The black helicopters will arrive shortly.

IF SOMEONE ELSE SHOOTS OR CLAIMS YOUR DEER:

Madness is an old Indian trick. The innocent natives believed that the gods protected the insane and left them alone. Most hunters believe there is a base level of civility and if that is obviously missing in your character, you will have the run of the woods. Nervous twitching, drooling, and wild rolling eyes all create nightmares for the pushy non-resident hunter.

Sportsmanship is the least effective judgment call. Game hogs have been cheating on their families and friends far too long in normal circumstances.

IF SOMEONE TAKES YOUR PARKING SPOT: Pull your old beater tight between their bumper and the road. Slap on stickers like "This

Car is protected by Smith and Wesson" and don't feed or water your blue heeler in the car. Leave one window open.

IF SOMEONE TAKES YOUR WOMAN: There is little chance of that happening because of your loving, caring, and nurturing relationship.

IF YOU WALK UP ON SOMEONE ELSE'S DEER: Clean the beast to the point of touching the really gross stuff. If they claim it, you don't have to do it. It's permissible to carve out a few filets for your trouble.

IF YOU HAVE AN UNRULY CAMP MEMBER: A party license will permit you to gut shoot a deer for their share.

WHERE TO HUNT

FEDERAL LAND: Saved for the hunting of immediate families of federal officers and political hacks on press junkets. These lands are managed by the Bureau of Land Management, the Forest Service, and the Corps of Engineers and are vast land holdings that, like an Annapolis appointment, require congressional approval to use the lodge.

MILITARY RESERVATIONS: Special permits require a short swearing-in ceremony, a short haircut, and custom clothing. The permits are good for two to four years.

PRIVATE TIMBER: If you own or plan to buy a wood frame house, it's generally okay to hunt acreage owned by the large timber companies. Hunt recently logged areas, as deer will congregate in the browse to eat the spotted owl carcasses found in large clear cuts.

STATE LAND: Saved for the exclusive hunting of the immediate families of state and local officials, including judges, justices of the peace, sheriffs, state patrolmen, and an occasional county permit clerk on the take. If another state borders your area, you may be in luck. Animals do not respect state lines except when crossing with another buck's doe.

STATE HUNTING AREAS: Where the deer and antelope do not play. In Texas, they took an aerial survey of the most inhospitable land combined with the fewest animals and reserved those 350,000 acres as a Wildlife Management Area/Public Hunting Lands Type II with special hunting fees.

POSTED, PRIVATE LAND: You need permission to hunt on posted land. Write, call, or just visit these yokels at home. If they can understand English, invite them to hunt with you. They especially like to drag out deer. Regulations say that your license doesn't authorize trespass but in some states the fine print shows that non-resident fees authorize a day hunt on posted land if, and only if, you close the gate behind you. If you see cattle at the gate, let them out as they too yearn to be free. If a farmer gives you written permission, that document is legal and can be passed on to your children and theirs as well. If the hunt didn't go well for whatever reason, photocopy and sell the permission slips to non-residents at the bar.

ASKING PERMISSION TO HUNT POSTED, PRIVATE LAND

It's better to ask for permission than beg for forgiveness (see section on treating gunshot wounds).

✔ *BEST HOURS TO ASK:* When the owners are awake. Farm families get up pretty early so just park in the driveway and wait until the bathroom light comes on before knocking on the door. If it's 3 AM, it may just be the farmer with a prostate problem. Wait until first light at least.

WAYS TO OVERCOME UNREASONABLE RESISTANCE

✔ *FOOD:* Where they don't get fresh food often, offer a case of c-rations. The peaches and pears in a sugar broth are pretty good, except for diabetics.

✔ *SOMETHING PRETTY FOR THE FARM WIFE:* A bolt of cloth or nylons without seams. If you plan to give undergarments, have plenty of the larger sizes because rural women have bigger poopers than their city sisters.

✔ *SOMETHING THEY CAN'T FIND AT THE FEED STORE:* A parrot, or better yet, a llama with hip dysplasia, or a stillborn pigmy dwarf goat.

After a great hunt, send something really expensive, like a gift certificate for chemotherapy or a hip replacement.

NEAR A PUBLIC GAME PRESERVE: Have your little lady organize a large Audubon birdwatching group on the preserve on opening day and post shooters at all four corners. Near a private exotic game preserve, you'll easily see the giraffes coming through the scrub brush.

IN A GAME MANAGEMENT AREA: Deer may be wearing radio collars so just listen for your favorite station. You are asked not to shoot deer with radios regardless of how loud they are playing. If by accident you bag a ghetto blaster, yell into the receiver to wake the survey crew on the other end.

IN TOWN: The best place to hunt, usually restricted to bow and arrow. City parks, water reservoirs, the police chief's backyard, school playgrounds, zoos after hours, and town squares should be hunted and hunted hard.

INDIAN RESERVATIONS: If you show receipts from tribal casinos and/or fireworks stands, you can hunt but only using traditional methods. Game taken from reservations must have an attached official tribal document such as a stone with a sharp edge, a beaded leather codpiece, or the keys to a Trans Am on blocks.

IN THE MOUNTAINS: If you have the legs of a billy goat and the stamina of a long distance runner, mountain hunting can be very productive, and done right, the critter will conveniently roll downhill to your pickup.

Conventional wisdom is to hunt a mountainside traversing at diagonals like these:

The object is to crisscross to a location above the deer, locate their bony heads with binoculars, and adjusting for altitude and angle, punch a hole in that mountain climber. Young bucks love to play King of the Hill so the object is to get to the top first. A deer will not sleep on the top of a mountain, as it can be very uncomfortable. You will have to get up very early to beat an animal used to playing this reign deer game.

WRONG WAY   RIGHT WAY

If it's your first time in the hills, the traversing will make you walk funny. If you don't walk short leg/long leg, you'll fall downhill.

If you walk only on one side of a mountain, your hips will slip out of alignment and lock, forcing you to forever walk with one foot off the curb.

IN SWAMPS: Nasty, stinky bogs full of snakes, leeches, and quicksand are where the really big bucks like Bambi's stag dad spend their retirement.

Informal surveys by Buck's friends have found racks in these golden ponds almost triple the largest known Boom and Crockpot heads, evidence of giants that have survived all trophy hunter tricks. The swamplands offer a large feast of plant life all year and efforts here will pay off.

A good pair of waders or a wet suit is recommended for swamp hunting and the best stand is an abandoned beaver house. The best way to find an empty hunter hotel is to convince your younger brother to bring his diving goggles during a preseason outing. Hold on to his feet for a quick pullout

should he bump into Bucky and Betty Beaver coming out and dressed to chomp through another forest. Crawl in and enlarge the inner cavity so the two of you can fit in there comfortably, back to back.

IN CORNFIELDS: Grain-fed deer is prized table meat. Deer feeding elsewhere on sagebrush, cacti, and salmon taste like what they eat. Used to seeing farm families in funny-looking clothing, corn-fed deer are almost tame and, if full of sweet corn, are easy to hunt. During preseason, scout with a farmer friend by riding along on field chores, looking for fresh sign. In season, strap yourself sidesaddle along the John Deere like an Indian on a painted pony and fill your crop-damage permits.

If your friend's farm machinery is tied up in bankruptcy court, practice still-hunting. To cornstalk, work a pattern back and forth, with the wind

blowing across at a ninety-degree angle. Always keep downwind, with the wind in your face. Keep facing the wind no matter what direction you catch yourself going.

Deer stands should be landmarks that deer can get used to seeing. Traditional approaches include tying cornstalks around your body or disguising yourself as a scarecrow.

Aggressive young farmers will race along the furrows with combines and binders, sweeping deer off their feet and baling the critters. Small deer can be easily picked up, while the larger deer must be lifted with help from the hired hands.

WHEN TO HUNT

THE BEST TIMES OF DAY TO HUNT

✔ *BEFORE DAYBREAK*: Some of the young bucks are just coming home so it's a good time to catch them with their buckskins down. The big bucks are snoozing away in the deep hollows, alpha-waving through their own stag movies, while does are trying to sneak out of the beds before the mature bucks rise. The reverse is true. Hunt the wiser does that wait until the big bucks go to bed.

✔ *SUNRISE TO MIDMORNING:* When old Sol climbs over the horizon, the grains of last night's feeding start swelling and deer bellies start rumbling. Deer will get up, stretch, and go check out any new arrivals to the neighborhood. If a non-resident hunter is stumbling into the woods, the deer will lie down, knowing he'll pass them by or move out, avoiding an accident.

✔ *MIDMORNING TO FIRST HUNGER PAIN:* Time is too short to be measured.

✔ *LUNCH HOUR:* Deer move at noon because they know you are busy. They can hear the pressure release of the coffee thermos, the crinkly potato chip bag, and the charcoal being dropped on the Weber grill. If the hunting area is near a factory town with a whistle or bell, the animals know exactly when the lunch bucket opens.

✔ *UP TO SIESTA TIME:* Deer move even more knowing that you overate and the high sun has warmed your inflated gut pile and dulled your senses.

✔ *TO DUSK:* Deer are getting ready for their evening strolls along the most popular game trails and may want to get an early start.

✔ *IN THE DUSK:* Don't worry about game wardens hearing your shots. Shoot three times even though you dropped that large shadow with one shot and yell out, "Help, I'm lost!" Gut quick and bury the carcass for a morning pickup.

THE BEST WEATHER TO HUNT

✔ *WARM AND SUNNY:* No matter what the old-timers say, more deer are taken in good weather than in bad, in warm sunny woods like the movies, or landscapes freshly painted by itinerant Impressionists.

In the North, game officials set the opening day after being assured by staff meteorologists that the rifle season will coincide with the first ice storm. Muzzleloaders and archers snooze away the earlier seasons under an oak tree, waiting for a deer with sunstroke to trip over them. Buck will do his preseason scouting during the warm months, wearing his natural deerskin moccasins stuffed with grass so deer will feel comfortable, smelling the skin tracks of their brothers and sisters.

In the South, when it gets too warm, Buck strips down to his shorts to hunt, making sure to wear shorts with a button fly, not metal fasteners or an open fly that will let the "Big Guy" get a sunburn. Open-toed sandals keep toes cool, and a hat is important to keep the sun from frying the throbbing network of veins on your nose. Buck's chest is covered with rich, black, curly hair so he'll weave in some twigs and leaves for natural camouflage. When you walk in the dusty soil, drag and kick your feet to create additional cover. In the lush Southeast, it's okay to wear Hawaiian shirts. Deer acknowledge fashion statements with quick, jerky nods of the head.

✔ *COLD AND STORMY:* When the barometer starts falling, deer start frenzy feeding, eating until they almost pop. Their stomachs will stretch, pressing their lungs north and their intestine south, producing short-winded, constipated, Type A personalities. Stand near these feeding areas but not too close because there are infrequent reports of thin-skinned big eaters exploding.

When a storm is about to hit, move to a location near the exit runways leading to the thick cover where they'll weather the storm. Buck stood through one of the worst opening day storms in northern Minnesota and saw a lot of deer movement in that horizontal sleet storm. At least they looked like deer. At least they were something large and stopped moving once a few shells were lobbed at them.

Deer don't care about the cold so much. They don't get hypothermia. Cool weather actually keeps their coats from sticking too close. High humidity combined with cold temperatures will freeze sleeping deer to the ground and the animals must wait for the sun to hit their slope to start the day.

✔ *IN REALLY COLD WEATHER,* deer pig-pile on top of each other for warmth, with the big bucks on top. By shooting the top animal, you'll not only have bagged the largest beast but the carcass will hold the others tight for your hunting buddies.

✔ *IN THE RAIN:* Heavy spring showers can bring on a whole rash of childhood ailments like bronchitis and croup. Light rain produces gray, depressing days for the animal and the waterlogged deer will become morose and aggressively introspective. The associated suicidal tendencies help the hunter willing to stand under an umbrella.

Rain will wash away many smells and the clear air makes the area much more dangerous for a deer. Deer will not bed in depressions in the rain and will look for higher, flatter, and dryer ground. There are rare occasions where deer have caught catnaps in the back of pickup trucks while their owners were standing, soaking wet, less than a hundred yards into the woods.

If caught in a thunderstorm, hold tight, taking care to keep your rifle barrel lower than your head. Electrical energy can flash across the sky to your iron peep sights and cause you to leave your tree stand early, much to the animal's amusement.

✔ *IN THE SNOW:* Snow will push deer up from lowlands and down from highlands. It's most irritating to deer to have Mother Nature hide food like this. Deer will paw their way down to the frozen foods. Frozen acorns are a very popular early evening snack (bucks like to hear them crack in their mouths) but most deer won't feed if the snow is blowing and covering their snacks. The bigger danger is the chance of frostbite of the nose while poking around in the freezer.

Foolish fawns have had their noses frozen from this error and soon the black tip, like frozen toes, will rot and fall off, leaving the deer a life of sinus headaches and bad colds.

Deer will move from one area when the natural snow depth reaches certain parts of their undercarriage. You know what part of the undercarriage I mean.

Some hunters say that falling snow makes deer blink more often and can cause rear-end accidents. Falling snow will muffle a hunter's footsteps and wise old bucks will lie down and curl up under the new white blanket. When you stalk in light snow, take care not to step on any large, live lumps.

✔ *GALE FORCE WINDS, HURRICANES, AND TORNADOES:* High, heavy winds are terrible to hunt in. Deer hunker down since the woods become too noisy, and thus dangerous. Gale and hurricane force winds in Florida will help in the hunting of the lightweight Key deer found in the south. You'll need to keep your upland bird shooting skills sharp to hit them.

During a tornado, deer huddle under trailer parks on the advice of unscrupulous mobile home salespeople. With the high center of gravity, deer caught out in the open are swept up off their feet and carried for many miles, often across state lines into unfamiliar surroundings.

Medium to light winds make deer act like airport windsocks, facing the winds sniffing for that garlic sandwich you had for lunch.

HOW TO HUNT

SPOTTING DEER: Deer are the only large thing moving about in the woods, except for a lost non-resident. You can hear them stumbling through the brush with flushing dogs hanging off their back legs, or maybe only the snap of a twig.

What you will rarely see, especially when hunting for whitetails, is a complete body. Experienced hunters look for pieces of deer, an antler here, a back there. Train your eyes to pick out abnormalities in the woods such as horizontals where only verticals should be, shiny antlers and wet runny noses. Moist eyes are a dead giveaway.

Remember that an ordinary deer in Wisconsin is not much larger than your neighbor's guard dog. If you shoot a deer as large as a horse, you have shot a horse. The most important clue is most deer are seen with their feet on the ground. It's very rare to see a deer in a tree unless it thinks it's a roosting turkey.

DEER CAMOUFLAGE: Deer colors are designed by Mother Nature to blend in with their immediate surroundings. They do have a few difficulties.

When they shed their summer coats, the naked animals seem embarrassed and lie dormant during this period. The new winter hair comes in early fall and is itchy during the first few weeks. The winter coats fall off in early spring and are quickly eaten by ground squirrels that enjoy the oversized hairballs.

If their coats change before the colors in the woods, the animal will stand out like brown shoes at a formal dance. The animals will once again go into seclusion until the colors coordinate.

Deer will do anything to break up their outline in the woods. They are commonly known to hide behind trees, brush, and non-residents.

What's not commonly known is that:

- ✔ Big deer will hide behind other animals. On a migration, a line of doe toe to tail will hide a big buck sneaking along the lee side of a hunter.
- ✔ Big deer will walk on their back legs but only for short distances because of their congenitally weak ankles.
- ✔ Big deer will stand on one leg like a stork if they can lean against a tree or another animal. Don't be fooled by this. There are few one-legged deer left except in Wisconsin where hunters full of "freshly brewed" stale local beer undershoot their animals.
- ✔ Deer will purposefully walk through brambles and thickets to pick up extra camouflage.
- ✔ Deer will stop licking their hair during the season, knowing that a spit-greased animal sticks out like a sore thumb.

BUCK'S BONUS TIP: The largest bucks have recognizable physical traits, like a big, deep chest, swayed back, potbelly, loose skin, enlarged prostate, and hemorrhoids. During the rut, their swollen neck folds into their full shoulders. A wallhanger's headgear can be measured in several ways. If the beam extends to the end of the nose, it's a keeper. If it goes much beyond that, you shot Rudolph instead. If the buck's rack substantially extends beyond the spread of alert ears, it's a keeper. Disregard if both ears are missing after the shotgun season in Wisconsin. Professional scorers add up totals. If your estimate of the tine, main beam, and spread length is two feet long, the buck is worth plugging if you can't find one measuring three feet long. If you find one over three feet long, pray you aren't in a ground stand covered with doe-in-heat urine.

JUDGING DISTANCE: There are range-finding devices on the market but Buck saves you money with an easy way to measure distance:

IF THE DEER LOOKS THIS BIG, IT'S 50 YARDS AWAY.

IF THE DEER LOOKS THIS BIG, IT'S 100 YARDS AWAY.

IF THE DEER LOOKS THIS BIG, IT'S A LONG WAYS AWAY.

AIMING AT DEER: You have to take a bead on a killing zone on the animal. Buck shows you where to aim on an animal and passes on the clue that anyone hunting with a responsible firearm will get more deer by "low punching" the chip off its shoulder. This knocks a deer down and keeps it down. Don't shoot at the heart. This is the best camp meat and not polite to the romantic thoughts harbored within. Don't try to shoot the antlers off as they come with the carcass.

The state sport in Wisconsin is to "shoot the flag," right up the O ring, carving out filets and popping the spinal cord as the already tired bullet falls out the mouth. This "banging the bung" is very embarrassing to the mature animal.

SHOOTING AT DEER: No way getting around it. The bullet will not leave the gun until the trigger is pulled, setting off a chain reaction with the firing pin hitting the primer and the shell exploding out the muzzle, looking for a warm body to blow apart.

The faster you pull the trigger, the faster the bullet will go out. On these fast trigger pulls, you risk pulling your aim and hitting the doe, but shoot before buck fever sets in or you may miss a buck/fawn combo.

If the deer is running, don't shoot. These animals are difficult to hit. It's best to wait until they stop. If you must shoot a deer on the run, lead the animal. A rule of thumb is to take the speed of the deer in miles per hour times how far the animal is away in yards, divide by the overall velocity of the bullet in yards per second, and multiply by the degrees in outside temperature. With this formula, you can figure out where they will be and just shoot at that spot. They'll be there in a minute.

If the deer is standing still, this is the position they expect to be shot in. Deer like to stand still. Mule deer think standing still actually hides them. The really dumb ones even stand out in the open fields. Pick your best shot and blast away. If you're shooting uphill, aim up to a foot higher since bullets will drop some, taking care not to shoot straight up unless you want to knock off your own hat. If shooting downhill, aim a little lower since early in the ejaculatory, the bullet will rise. If you can't quite see the deer on the other side of the ridge, lob a few rounds over at a forty-five degree angle.

If the deer is lying down, shame on you for thinking to shoot the critter in its own bed. Wait until the animal wakes in its own good time and well into its early morning exercises.

If the deer is kneeling, make sure the posture is not some sort of animal genuflection to an animal god. It's not smart to interrupt a religious ceremony in the animal kingdom.

HOW TO SHOOT A WEAPON

✔ *STANDING UP:* The most difficult shooting position. Buck uses a very long sling he can step on to steady his shot. Walk past a deer holding tight, put your rifle over your shoulder, aim backwards toward the spot the buck is lying, and pull the trigger. Shooting without a brace is called "shooting off hand." This is not to be confused with shooting your hand off. See section on hunting with handguns.

✔ *SITTING OR KNEELING:* The closer you get to the ground, the steadier the shot. If you hadn't noticed, squatting (called the "Big Grunt") is the most vulnerable position and, once mastered, makes you completely prepared to shoot in the woods, regardless of where your pants are.

✔ *LYING DOWN:* If you believe like Buck this is the only good position, whether in a tree stand or not, practice getting down as often as you can. If you are a vet, it's easy. If you are a draft dodger, practice falling forward with a loaded piece. This position is more difficult with a bow and arrow. It can be done lying flat on your back.

As in all positions, use a bench rest, and that's another reason to have a woman hunting with you. Have her stretch out, belly down, in front of you and rest your large bore on her small bore. She'll appreciate the opportunity to help you score.

WHAT TO SHOOT

Trophy bucks are not:

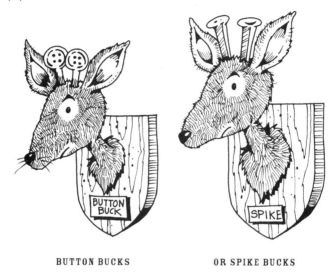

BUTTON BUCKS **OR SPIKE BUCKS**

Trophy bucks have monster heads sporting mega-racks that trophy hunters spend all of their waking hours stalking to get recorded in some dusty book called Boom and Crockpot (firearms) or Poop and Young (bow and arrow). Named after the two flashy cops on *Miami Vice*, Boom and Crockpot applicants are required to sign an affidavit swearing they fairly chased the animals through ten miles of bramble. Some states have their own Big Book and it is jealously guarded by game officials who enter non-resident heads in pencil, not ink, to be erased once a local good old boy bangs a larger head.

You can score your own animal if you are able to understand the complicated point system or ask an official B and C scorekeeper to determine if your animal can be entered into the headgear hall of fame. If you're really pressed for time, send the entire head to the club. They'll clean it up for you and send back a mounted skull with a nice certificate. If you don't like the taste of venison, send the entire carcass. They'll appreciate the kindness.

Like their politicians, East Coast hunters exaggerate the size of their accomplishments by counting both sides of the head. In the West, the left side is the only count. If you shot a buck whose rack measures, by your count, over two hundred inches on one antler, you most likely shot a unicorn, which was not in season, to say the least.

Trophy does are a convenient fallback for hunters who pass the buck. A new national club, Masters of the Matriarch, tallies teats for the record book. Their thicker ankles, saggy skin, and big, floppy bags identify the old does.

Trophy fawns are a sophistication of the hunt for camp meats. Only those fawns with spots that measure three inches across can compete for these honors.

HITTING A DEER: You can tell that you actually hit a deer if you hear a loud splat (rifle or shotgun). The rubber suction cup on the tip of non-resident arrows bounces off a thick deer coat. When hit by such an arrow, deer typically turn their heads to where the thump came from and grunt, "Now what the hell?"

If you are a muzzleloader, wait until the smoke clears before proceeding. If you are a firearm shooter, wait until the ringing in your ears stops. If you are an archer, start reeling in your arrow. A tug on the line means meat on the table.

When you reach the spot where you hit the deer and it's lying on the ground, make sure it's dead before you start carving out the chops. Lean over and listen for a heartbeat or pick up a leg and check for a pulse. If there is a slight pulse, time is running out. Gently hold one hand over the mouth and nose, and pull the lids down over the sad eyes. If the deer has just been stunned, take off your belt and tie it on like a bridle, leading the dazed critter out to the road where you can finish it off near the truck.

If the deer isn't there, you may have missed altogether or blown it to kingdom come or the deer, though hit, may have taken off to die more deer-like elsewhere. Tracking skills aren't difficult to learn. Just follow the blood trail slowly, looking for telltale signs of a wound, such as chunks of hair, in Wisconsin a leg or tail, or if a fawn, some spots. Take fifteen-minute breaks. Tracking is easy in the snow and more difficult in a late fall woods. You are getting close when the hoof prints turn into knee prints. Dispatch a wounded critter quickly so the other worry-wart woodland creatures like Pepe Le Fart Sac and Winnie the Poop can go about their mindless animal ways.

BUCK'S BONUS TIP: Veteran deer will try to trick you. Having dodged your arrows and bullets, they limp away to lure a novice into a deeryard where the whole herd can rush you. These vets are known to even give themselves a bloody nose to make a trail.

✔ *FIELD DRESSING:* Gut your animal as close to a non-resident stand as you can without them noticing. If done right, this procedure is fast and easy. Buck has gutted a deer in less than three minutes and has won awards at the national Gut-a-Ramas sponsored by the knife manufacturers. Gutting is easy, just turn the insides out. Open the animal from belly button north and pull out anything not looking like a steak. Split the pelvic bone so the back legs can go akimbo. Go as far as you can into the neck. You'll know you've gone far enough when your hand comes out the mouth. Which may remind you of a favorite childhood hand puppet. If you were raised by a she-wolf.

✔ *GUT PILES:* If you've done your shooting and cleaning properly, all the guts will be in a nice wrapped pile on the ground. A large deer's gut pile will be big enough for a small kid to jump on and will make all sorts of neat sounds when they do. Any size gut pile is a nice handwarmer on a cold Minnesota morn.

What to do with it? Some leave the gut pile for the night animals and survivalists to eat. Some will bury it away from the prying eyes of hunting partners and game officials. It is important to take what you can from this shopping bag of fine meats, in particular the heart and liver. These are considered prime camp meats and part of a traditional first night's meal at camp. Buck will usually leave the other parts where they lie unless there is a homeless charity drop box nearby.

BUCK'S BONUS TIP: Most state laws require you to place your hunting tag on a downed animal before moving it. The only exception is when you shot the wrong animal, like a fawn. Just drag and cover it with leaves near a non-residents' stand when they are taking a nap in the RV. And call the warden with their stand co-ordinates.

BUCK'S EXTRA BONUS TIP: Decide whether to take out the deer then or wait for help the next day. If you opt to leave the animal in the woods, protect your interests by whizzing a scent trail around the carcass. If it's a non-resident's animal and there's a chance of wolves in the area, it's considered good sportsmanship to leave a Big Job direct-ly on the carcass.

TAKING A DEER OUT OF THE WOODS: You are a non-resident rube if you shoot down into a valley. The deer won't come up and die at your feet—they'll find a deeper crevasse to fall into. Shoot an animal close to the road; veteran deer try to die as far from your truck as possible. At some point, you have to get your deer out of the woods. You can take the whole thing by dragging or carrying. The most common drag is a drag. You'll soon learn why deer prefer to walk out of the woods.

For carrying, an Indian-style travois remains a favorite. It is, after all, the way a junior member of the camp brought you in.

Another familiar method is to put the animal on a stick and carry the carcass between two people. Two hunters using this method invented Ben-Gay.

Most important, get someone else to take your deer out to the road.

> **_BUCK'S BONUS TIP:_ Savvy old-timers will field dress their animal into pieces and take the best parts out first. Once discovered so mutilated, these critters are evidence of an alien invasion and another good reason to raise non-resident fees.**

Before you cut it up, undress the critter by removing its buckskin jacket. The skin can be pulled off by hanging the animal upside down in a tree, cutting around its legs and stomach, and jumping off the tree, pulling the skin as you fall.

HOW TO WEIGH YOUR DEER

- ✔ *LIVE WEIGHT* refers to the walking pounds. Mule deer weigh a couple hundred pounds and whitetails less.
- ✔ *DEAD WEIGHT* is what's being carried or dragged by the hunter and, midway out of the woods, is calculated at twice the live weight. The term dead weight can also refer to your wife's family but that term should be used sparingly, especially at family reunions.

✔ *DRESSED WEIGHT* includes the hide but not the gut pile and is about eighty percent of the live weight.

✔ *BUTCHERED WEIGHT* is without the bones and junk and, depending on what a person calls junk, can be one half the live weight.

✔ *DINNER PLATE WEIGHT* is judged by the acceptance around the family table, and averages two pounds per animal.

BUTCHERING: This is the fun job. You'll learn what makes animals tick. You'll also learn how seriously overpaid union butchers are. Once you have the hair coat off, the critter looks like below but without the dotted lines and names.

Chop it up like shown below, wrap in double freezer paper, and mark accordingly. Grind any leftovers into hamburger and sausage.

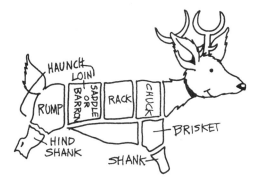

If you keep the head facing in the right direction, the other side will look exactly the same. Turn it over and complete the job.

If you don't have a dog, break the bones and bury in a non-hunter's flowerbed, and call the police homicide tip line.

YIELD

How much meat you get from a deer depends on the size and condition of the animal. Buck gets more meat because he slays larger deer and proportions change in super-bucks. For example, if Buck's buck had a dressed weight of 200 pounds, the yield would be roughly 150 pounds.

Roasts: 45 pounds
Steaks: 25 pounds
Chops: 25 pounds
Stew meat/burger: 30 pounds
Heart/liver/camp meat: 5 pounds
Nuts/testicles: 5 pounds (see Rocky Mountain oysters)
"Johnson" w/bone in: 15 pounds

If Buck's magnum reloads blew through the buck and knocked down the big doe behind, replace above nuts/testicles with breast meat (see succulents).

If the shell blew through the doe and knocked down the twin fawns hiding behind Mom, replace gender detail above with spots and eyelashes and don't tell your hunting partners. They don't deserve a lick of these prime edibles.

HOW TO DETERMINE THE AGE OF YOUR DEER: Official party line says you have to stick your head in a dead deer's mouth to count and judge the wear on the molars. Buck simply cuts through a leg bone to count the rings. Deer live about seven years if left alone, so figure one deer year is worth twelve people years in the US, five years and a half-rack of Molson's in Canada.

YOU AND THE STRONG ARM OF THE LAW

BEFORE THE HUNT: It's time to buy a license and read the regulations. You'll need to memorize the arcane rules that govern even your preseason activity. For example, it's illegal to put a permanent stand on government lands or in less permanent trees. You can't build corrals. You can't do this. You can't do that. It's like living at home all over again. Move out, Pilgrim!

DURING THE HUNT: Hunting regulations are very clear on how many deer you can shoot, with what, and on what days. The real confusion comes in the proper hours of shooting. As complicated as game officials make them, you might as well hunt by tide charts. You can safely shoot a little before sunrise and a little after sunset. If you hear hunters shooting earlier or later, they are probably doing some target practice. If you hear non-residents shooting in similar fashion, they are probably lost. Or still drunk. Never mind.

If you shoot an animal with a radio-collar, remove and attach to the outside of your car for the drive home. The game biologist on duty watching the big electronic map will think another deer has gone over the hill. If you bag several collars, it's possible to lure entire undergraduate study teams right into the city.

AFTER THE HUNT: Once your deer is tagged and ready to take home, you have just one legal hurdle to hop—the game check station. In most states, you must bring the game to the station by 8 PM or call the warden at home and promise to stop back in the morning. If you are a non-resident, you can leave your animal near the station's front door and be first in line the next morning. Game check stations are along all major roads pointing home and often disguised as game biologist checkpoints whose staff will ask you seemingly innocent questions. Evidence of the sex of your animal must be presented. If you blew the head off, one of more of the following things must be attached: penis, testicles, scrotum, and/or udder. If you are handy with a needle and thread, stitch a scrotum on a dry doe, especially if the biologist is an intern from a famous eastern school. If they can't tell what sex your animal is and you are hunting in a single sex license area, the biologist will scold you and make you take the deer back to where you found it.

In some states, all that's required is to drive by the game check station and honk as often as the number of deer you have crammed in the trunk—long honks for bucks, short beeps for fawns. In other states, you will have to stop so game biologists can cut the backstrap for their home studies on population densities.

Some states require a stop at the checking station even if you don't have an animal. This is so the officials can have a nice chat and serve the complimentary goodies your license paid for. In the morning, coffee, juice, and donuts are the usual fare, Midday offers a nice light sandwich and cup of soup, and in the evening, it's local beers, pretzels, and hardboiled eggs. If the goodies aren't on the front counter, they're in the back. The officials are such kidders. Keep pushing them. It's part of your hunting rights.

 BUCK'S BONUS TIP: You have the right in most states to make a citizen's arrest should you suspect a wrongdoing. Carry the largest weapon in these cases, seize the evidence, and tell the non-resident lawbreakers you'll be right back with a warrant for their arrest.

GAME WARDENS: Game wardens work for us taxpayers and, as busy as they are, they like to be reminded who their real employers are. The warden knows where the game is, so if there is a handsome single member of your party and the local warden has a daughter who's vulnerable due to her looks, unsettled marriage, or impending critical mass birthday, it doesn't hurt to gather a little information by penetration behind enemy lines.

Wardens will often give confiscated game or "mistake kills" to needy or empty-handed hunters. These animals are hanging in the warden's garage so visit early in the season while the good cuts are still available. Ask the warden if you can join him and his little woman for dinner to sample the goods. Be thoughtful. A warden's wife would appreciate a store-bought gift of some sort, like a book on log cabin feng shui, chocolate-covered Rocky Mountain oysters, or a bonus-sized can of Cheese-Whiz ®.

Game wardens get their legal authority from assorted hanging judges, and in many states are no longer required to wear uniforms. They can be identified only by their well-fed appearance. If they do wear uniforms, notice how formal they look. If they look like stormtroopers with high-gloss leather and a Smokey the Bear hat, don't hunt in their state. Ditto for the states that employ volunteer Guardian Angels. Younger wardens are graduates of different mail order courses on game conservation and, as graduates, have pledged to produce the gilt-edged diploma when asked.

Wardens know all the game laws. If you're shooting suds with pals at the Dew Drop Inn the night before the hunt and you have any questions, call the warden at home and be sure to let him know who's calling so he can thank you properly for your lawfulness in the stand next morning. It's likely he just got in from spending the wee hours posting "Open For Hunting" signs on game reserves, and is always happy to chat before settling down with the little lady who always wanted him to work for her father.

WRITTEN AND UNWRITTEN LAWS OF THE WOODS: The words a warden can use to hang your personal antlers on his office wall come in the form of printed regulations. Each state has its own booklet of shameful secrets and unmentionable customs and will send you a copy if asked. If they don't want out-of-state hunters or Yankee hunters yearning to blast below the Mason-Dixon Line, your request will go unanswered, be sent back without stamps, or answered "regretfully out of stock" and told to check back later in the year.

The regs are printed with the smallest type possible on paper that smears easily. In North Dakota, regs are called proclamations due to the very large population of Missouri Synod Lutherans hunting there. These thin documents are what the wardens pull out when your few rights are being read to you. Here they hide the nonsense about not being able to hunt on Sunday. Can you imagine the chaos if deer start understanding what the difference is between weekdays and weekends? We'd never get them to act like deer on Saturday either. The Hawaiians have it together by requiring hunting on weekends only. The regs include definitions of residency requirements, bag limits, and license types. Some states invent bag success ratios for each county to trick hunters into areas where there is low employment.

Generally speaking, if it's not prohibited, it's okay. For example, it's fairly clear that you can hunt deer with falcons. Tip: You'll need more than one.

You need to have some kind of license to hunt deer. Locals buy their permits in sporting goods and hardware stores. Game officials pick the most frequented public spots, so in Wisconsin licenses are sold only in breweries.

There are several common types of licenses:

✔ *RESIDENT:* Reserved for those who have religiously bought tickets to the game warden's ball, have wanted to live in the state for a long time, wear mismatched camouflage, and lived at least six months in a nice house with a well-kept lawn.

✔ *NON-RESIDENT:* Must have three major credit cards with high lines of credit and send a certified check six months before what's laughingly called an impartial drawing. (In Colorado, if you aren't drawn one year, you get one accumulated point and two John Denver records. Extra points come from special relationships with certain game officials, and contributions to political campaigns. These points are added up for the season's draw.)

    When applying for a non-resident license, the most common mistake is to underpay. Start off right and send an extra fifteen-percent as a gratuity to establish a long-term relationship. You don't have to be too clear on where you want to hunt. They'll give you the benefit of the doubt.

✔ *SPORTSMAN:* Reserved for special game management area hunts where special stamps or permits are required. Sportsmen must exceed all accepted standard sportsmanlike behavior in these areas.

✔ *FAMILY FARM:* If you are a landowner, you can shoot as many deer as you can eat in two sittings. If you are a renter or sharecropper, your limits are the same percentages as your land lease reads. If you learn that a family farm is getting federal tax incentives, you as a taxpayer can hunt that farm without asking and enjoy the same limits.

✔ *FELONS:* As an ex-con, you are not supposed to possess, much less carry a firearm. In some states, however, you are allowed to hunt with your parole officer, but only the parole officer gets to have bullets.

✔ *YOUTH:* In most states you have to be at least fourteen years old to hunt big game. This is validated by the ratio of acne to smooth surfaces on face and neck. A youth must be a graduate of an expensive hunter safety class given by retired game officials that never liked hunters to begin with.

✔ *LIFETIME:* In Texas, you can buy a lifetime license even though there is no good reason to spend a lifetime there. These licenses are real moneymakers for states with high accident rates. The license is buried with the deceased if there is room in the casket after the widow stuffs it full of the old bastard's hunting junk. If the deceased was deceased because of a hunting accident or a case of buck fever, the family is entitled to a free deer crossing sign for use as a grave marker.

✔ *DEPRIVATION:* When animals multiply too fast, game officials declare emergency hunts and allow hunters with fully automatic weapons to thin the ranks. All prohibitions are waived and all inhibitions are lost in these hunting horror scenes.

✔ *MILITARY:* Reserved for active duty personnel only, unless you're still able to squeeze into your dress khakis. The highest kill ratio is on military reservations housing armored and artillery divisions where there is a choice of their weapons.

✔ *SENIOR:* If you are over sixty-five, most states will let you hunt free, but you can't go deep into the woods. If you are particularly forgetful, a special senior's warden will stop by to check your survival equipment before you go into the woods.

✔ *PARTY:* These permits allow you to hunt with others and shoot each other's deer. You can shoot a doe for a trophy buck hunter friend, and, if the rest of the party is filled out, that's the deer he has to take home. A party permit for four Wisconsin sportsmen will get four permits and a six-pack of Schlitz. They have to drink the Schlitz. Party licenses are sold behind the bars of 3.2 taverns all over the Midwest, right next to the pickled eggs.

Every license includes a tag to attach to your downed animal. This tag must be attached immediately after you shoot the animal and stay attached until you eat the whole thing. It's not as difficult as it sounds. For example, when you are boiling a leg in a pot on the stove, hang the tag over the side like a tea bag.

In a few states, licenses are sewn on to the back of a jacket or cap, in full view so the warden can glass you from afar.

The big game license in some states is the senior license, and allows you to take as many smaller game animals as you can stuff into the deer's belly cavity. This deer license also allows you to take a bear if the bruin gets to your deer first and doesn't want to share.

In Maryland you can apply for a big game license but must hunt with a "socially acceptable" weapon, following a lengthy approval process led by two schoolmarms, a crossing guard, librarian, victim of a gun crime, and a billy goat.

If you forget your license, wardens normally carry extras. Ask for one so you can tag your deer. In the more service-minded states, and at this printing there are none, they will take plastic. It's also very thoughtful to offer a cash tip for all their help. In Maine, wardens will cash checks, up to $200 for out-of-towners, with two pieces of I.D.

✔ *IMPORTANT REMINDER:* You can get a refund on a license if the game department made an error like misspelling your name, mistaking your sex, or housing you at the wrong address. Some unscrupulous sportsmen will return their unfilled tags claiming small errors. Shame on them. Refunds are also available if you die before the season starts. If you die of buck fever midseason, you'll get only half your money back.

 BUCK'S BONUS TIP: Tag your buck in a spot that game wardens don't like to touch. You know where! Down there!

Fill your pen with invisible ink and let your partners use it before driving off to check into a game station.

HOW SEASONS, LIMITS, AND GENDER RULES ARE SET:

Seasons are determined by the general activity of the deer and the desired harvest determined by game biologists. The recommendations are then passed to the head of the state game department where they decide on a number to compete with their buddies from nearby states. There is a lot of one-upsmanship as they scheme for the non-resident dollar. They will hold back publication of their own regulations until they can see what the neighboring states are doing. Without competitive information, the game heads use random means like dartboards to set season limits. Buck has inside knowledge that Wisconsin game officials use the urinal roulette wheels attached to the blue deodorizers. For those not familiar with Wisconsin, it's behind you if you are facing the Dakotas. If you face the Dakotas too close in January, your nose and any other unprotected appendage will freeze off.

Game limits are at best general guidelines. In many states, it's the spirit of the law rather than the letter that is enforced. Call ahead to the game department to find out which states these are. If you are allotted one big buck per year, this limit can be filled with two spike bucks or one doe and a fawn. In several states, one doe is worth two fawns since twins are common in healthy herds and the spots are easy to draw a bead on.

Gender limits are used to balance a herd out. If there are too many does, they tend to get crabby and picky about everything and should be thinned out. If there are too many bucks, the does complain about the pressure to satisfy the lust of the bucks and they, too, have to be weeded out. The best way to thin bucks out is to open their season when they are the hormonal heavies of the rut.

RULES OF BLAZE ORANGE:

Except for a few small new irritants, like having to buy habitat stamps for special game management areas, there hasn't been much new in regs for years. Buck has uncovered a scheme by several mountain states to add a migratory stamp for shooting mulies that move from one food plot to another during heavy snows. This measure is small change compared to the laws regarding blaze orange, specifically designed to fill the low occupancy of poacher prisons.

Game biologists, wardens, and retail clothing manufacturers have conspired to produce a report saying that blaze orange is the most visible color in the woods and require that a certain amount of this obnoxious color be worn during your hunt. Blaze orange is already a trade name. What does that tell you? Many states don't even allow the more fashionable blaze orange camo. The only exceptions to these blaze orange rules are for farmers hunting on their own property and bowhunters, again evidence of the powerful, colorful lobbies in Congress.

The language is noticeably ambiguous in most regs and very specific in some. It's hard to say which is worst. In Wisconsin, the language is loose but ominous: "Faded or food, urine, or poop (number 2) stained blaze orange clothing is unsafe and MAY NOT meet law requirements."

The minimum requirements are at least some orange, visible from all sides. The square inch requirement runs from 150 to 500 square inches, worn above the beltline. The madness hits its logical extreme in Maine where they have forced hunters to buy fresh gear each year from overpriced mail order catalogs because of regulations like these:

"Anyone who hunts with a firearm during open firearm season on deer is required to wear an article of solid-colored hunter orange clothing with a dominant wave length between 595 and 605 nanometers, excitation purity not less than 85 percent, pubescent purity of 80 percent, and luminance factor of not less than 40 percent."

Now Buck asks you—Have you had your clothing wavelengths measured lately? Just go to our country's answer to Finland and have one of their junior birdmen quick-draw a nanometer on you.

MISTAKE KILL: If you or your hunting partner mistakenly kill any game you shouldn't have, most state laws require you to remove the entrails and deliver the carcass to the local game warden, who will try to eat the meat before next weekend. This restitution should be made within ten days as most wardens like a little aging on their meat.

If the accident is an extra deer or a wrong sex deer, don't try to cover it up or cache it away for next season. Leave the animal on the warden's doorstep when he's not home. Strip out the backstrap and attach a note saying the coyote got to the carcass first.

If the accident involves a cow, horse, or llama, you may be in trouble. Check the brand so you know who will be the plaintiff if you are observed stripping out the prime fillets. Llama meat isn't fit to eat unless your family hauls coffee beans in the Andes.

If the accident is an elk, moose, bear, or any endangered species, you are in bigger trouble. You've committed a big no-no. Even your long family history of mental illness won't help. You and your next generation will lose hunting privileges, and always remain a non-resident in your own state. You'll be stripped of your legal and illegal firearms, and the epaulettes of your new safari shirt will be ripped off. They will take your wheels and you'll have to catch a bus home. Before the ink from your fingerprints is dry, the game wardens will go into your house and confiscate your trophy wall, and make a serious pass at your wife who is probably in a motel room with the lawn boy anyway. You'll never be able to wear blaze orange again except to Denver Bronco games. Your last deer stand will be on the reserved bench outside the whitetail display at the zoo. Life as you know it will come to a halt.

POACHING: Poaching deer is not a method of cooking, it's illegally taking deer that rightfully should be running by your stand. Recent evidence uncovered in Miami suggests that most poaching is run by out-of-country "save the little people" funds, headquartered in Colombia or Nicaragua. These organizations have U.S. drop boxes in Delaware, and are funded by empty-nester contract hunters to illegally harvest large herds. This enables them to force feed red meat to Third World children. It's been medically proven that unwashed rice with large chunks of venison is the best diet to produce healthy adult cocaine smugglers.

Other poaching is done by those chumps in your high school class who still can't read road signs or who, in their quiet times in the tin trailer with a

longneck beer, still think that school rules don't apply to them. These people have their original crew cuts, widely spaced crossed eyes, and bad teeth, and consider their three-legged dog their best friend.

Poaching for antlers is for only the lowest of the low. Knowing that ground-up antlers are sold as an aphrodisiac, poachers will slay animals for their headgear alone. Game geneticists are racing to produce an animal whose antlers will cause citywide impotence in many Asian cities.

Poachers are fined restoration penalties to replenish herds and these charges, tacked on top of the fines imposed by courageous circuit judges and justices of the peace with humongous walk-in game-meat lockers, total up to $25 US or $7,000 Canadian per person.

Poaching is usually done with spotlights that make a large animal's legs lock tight. In high poaching areas, drive to your stand with only the parking lights on so the warden doesn't mistake your high beams for a pair of poaching spotlights.

✔ *POACHING AS A LIVING:* Subsistence hunting is a specialized type of poaching practiced most commonly in Alaska and other desolate areas by shirt-tail relatives of proud natives who settled the land or dropouts from traditional longhouse get-togethers. These accomplished hunters use the traditional hunting weapons of their ancestors, such as snowmobiles, air-powered boats, and fully automatic weapons, and harvest enough food for a season weekly.

The original treaty rights negotiated by courageous lawmakers grant natives large harvests but today's natives are larger eaters than their ancestors. Based on their per capita harvest, each native eats over five hundred pounds of venison a week, averaging twenty-three pounds per meal, more on the larger Sunday potlatches.

A few subsistence hunters are back to nature enthusiasts, people on the lam from the alimony bounty hunters of Texas and Oklahoma, and who feel in the tradition of Jack London that giving up the comforts of civilization has earned them the right to pretty much eat as they go along. Buck has researched this guy London and learned that not only did he not like to eat venison, but all those tales of the North were actually written in a north-end San Francisco hotel and the famous dog stories were actually about a bad-tempered Chihuahua London kept under his bed.

 BUCK'S BONUS TIP: With the interest by restaurants in wild-lite game meals, make sure you aren't ordering venison medallions from a poached animal. Politely, but firmly demand that the frog waiter hovering over the low neckline of your little woman produce a bill of sale from a reputable game farm. If he's unable to do so, leave loudly, using these French words of civic concern: "Hé, merde, ça schlingue ici! Y'a un salaud qui a pété! C'est degueulasse, je vais dégobiller. Les français sont tous de phallos! Connard! Va te faire foutre!"

WHERE WARDENS RETIRE—CONFISCATION HOMES:

Scattered through hunting states are state owned and operated homes to let wardens spend their last years free from the threats of poaching cabals. Wardens are recommended to a home when there are collaborating reports of unusual behavior. If when confronting a hunter, a warden displays trembling hands, sweat on the brow, and dilated pupils, and/or gasps audibly once the animal is confiscated, he is a likely candidate.

From the street they resemble large retirement homes, built as a hollow square with ample hunting habitat in the middle. The inner square is designed for staff who dress as hunters and carry illegal game back and forth so the residents can keep their skills sharp. The dining hall is decorated like a small-town cafe, with counter service and older women dressed in short, white dresses, answering to names like Dottie, Ruby, and Mabel. The coffeepot is always on. One half hour before sunrise until one half hour past sunset, the staff plays hunting cassettes taped at a local rifle range. Quiet environmental tapes accompany the dark hours. The front rooms facing the street are the preferred views and have crank-open windows for any deer drives that take place. Game warden fines and the United Way support these homes.

HUNTING IN CANADA:

Regulations take on a new meaning north of the border as you try to take your favorite weapon across the line.

✔ *WHAT'S PROHIBITED:* Fully automatic rifles and machine guns, sawed-off shotguns, switchblades, silencers, mace, throwing stars, nunchaku sticks, belt buckle knives, spiked waistbands, blowguns, or brass knuckles. (The last prohibited item is specific to "made men" and the focus of a class action suit filed in New Jersey.)

✔ *WHAT'S RESTRICTED:* (With permits only) one-hand firearms (pistols, etc.), short semi-automatics like carbines, Uzi semiautomatics if brought in for specific competitions, and terrorist class and special class rifles.

✔ *WHAT'S PERMITTED:* Long guns are okay to import if you have the weapon broken down and stored in different parts of the car. Put the barrel in trunk, stock in back seat, bolt in glove box, and bullets in the ashtray. You must have the same number of bullets as the number of licenses, and at least $500 in hard currency and promise to spend it all while there.

Once you are in country, you fall into one of three categories: resident, non-resident, or non-Canadian, each with separate permits. The limits are similar and the prices are fairly reasonable especially knowing the prices aren't in real dollars. Do not make comments about the RCMP uniforms at checkpoints, no matter how goofy Sergeant Preston might look or remark, "My how big a flea collar" is on Yukon King.

Provincial officials make their own hunters feel good about their sport by making them buy various permits.

✔ *PERMIT TO CONVEY:* Required in order to take a restricted firearm, like a pistol, from where it was purchased to the local registrar of firearms for registration, even if it's the next counter down.

✔ *PERMIT TO TRANSPORT:* Required in order to take a restricted weapon from home to the repair shop and return, with a solemn promise not to shoot anything on the way.

✔ *PERMIT TO CARRY:* Required in order to possess a pistol at the firing range, even if it's to keep the spectators in line.

The provinces have their own special requirements.

In Nova Scotia, no hunter can take more than fifteen pounds of his deer to a neighbor unless the recipient has a valid storage permit issued by the health department and is a good neighbor. You also have to eat your deer by April 30 of the following year or apply for a storage permit, which is seldom given unless the hunter has a good reason for not eating freezer-burned meat.

Guides in the province are not allowed to guide more than three American hunters or twenty-five other Canadian hunters. No hunter can go into the woods unless "that person possesses a compass in working order and able to operate said compass to the satisfaction of any uniformed provincial employee not on strike."

In Manitoba, deer hunters can only include up to four people in a hunting party. Over four, you are considered an unruly mob (similar to their political parties) and subject to police harassment.

You are also asked to donate the reproductive tracts of the females. It is not clear what game officials do with these but the request smacks of improper behavior. The wardens even ask that you donate the hindquarters and back-strap for cadmium studies, whatever cadmium is. If you cooperate, you have a chance in a prize drawing for one hundred pounds of baby seal meat and a bottle of Canadian wine, whatever Canadian wine is.

In Ontario, the game seal must be locked through the cartilage separating the nostrils, similar to the locking nose devices that larger Ontario women use on their men. Only residents get to hunt does. Since there are no limits to the number of dogs you can use to hunt deer, all the nightmares animal rights activists have about this blood sport take place in Ontario. You can get a special souvenir hunting cap with polar bear cub fur-lined earflaps from the ministry in exchange for a suitably prepared deer hide for native peoples. The license holder must chew these hides properly but the caps are well worth the effort. However, the caps do not have a bill on them as there was confusion as to what side they should go.

In British Columbia, dogs must be on a leash and the leash must be tied to the belt buckle of the hunter. Leashes cannot exceed 100 feet. In the la-la land of Western Canada, you can take fawn mule deer as camp snacks if you have a special limited entry hunting authorization, whatever that is. If you hunt within one hundred kilometers of Victoria, you're expected to bring the field dressed carcass to the tenth floor of the government building so it can be checked off in the big book. Please use the service elevator.

In Alberta, you cannot shoot more than 200 rounds of ammo per deer. Per day. Unless they are bedded down for the night.

In Saskatchewan, you cannot "aid or assist a Treaty Indian who is hunting for food in accordance with treaty rights unless you are also a Treaty Indian." Between the lines, this means dressed and acting like a Treaty Indian, which includes most Canadian sportsmen.

If you have failed to retrieve a wounded animal after emptying your quiver, you can use your archer's license for the firearms season, but only accompanied by another hunter who has actually shot a deer with a rifle.

All hunters of this province must wear "a complete outer suit of scarlet, bright yellow, blaze orange, or white or any combination of these colors. Your cap must be any one of these except white." These authorized colors allow the successful hunter to go directly to the golf course without changing clothes.

The Fair Trade agreement requires Canadians to keep the hindquarters of each Canadian deer as it's the only international transaction they won't lose their arse in.

It is absolutely prohibited for Canadians to hunt while under the influence of American-made beer or liquor. It's also a misdemeanor under Canadian Code of Bar Ethics for an American to question or appear to slander the source of the water in Canadian beer. Brewpubs in Canada are prohibited from using toilet or urinal water in their brewing process (unless in drought conditions at which time Canadian "blue" becomes available on grocer's shelves).

GOING HOME

TAKING A DEER HOME: Many states require a public display of your animal, in part because of smuggling and also as a lesson to other large animals. There are as many ways to display an animal as there are means of transport.

✔ *BY CAR OR TRUCK:* Some hunters like to precook their animal by putting it over the front of their car. A warm engine in a warm climate will cook a full-size deer medium-rare in under a hundred miles. Turn the carcass every twenty-five miles.

✔ *BY TRAIN:* The smaller lines have limited baggage room but are less formal. Don't skin the animal. Wrap the body tight with duct tape, strapping the feet tightly down, and shove the animal in the overhead compartment. Jam the tongue back in the mouth and tape it shut. Close the crossed eyes so as not to offend the other passengers.

✔ *BY PLANE:* Airline people don't like hunters to begin with but what can you expect from people who lived on left-behind airline food. They always make you open the gun case that you have bound tight with duct tape. To make it worth their while, buy an extra gun case and carry the gut pile in that one.

Buck debones a deer wherever he hunts and packs it cleans and double-wrapped in a heavy-duty garbage bag inside a stiff, two-suiter. He will keep a few pieces out for a quick pick-me-up between the five-course trail mix meals on board.

✔ *BY COURIER:* Sensing an opportunity, several overnight carriers have told Buck that they'll soon offer a special "game bag" that can go directly to your wife so she can clean and wrap the meat before you get home. If you want the meat aged, ship UPS Ground.

EATING YOUR DEER: You are at home and again the provider. If you followed Buck's advice, you have anywhere from 50 to 150 pounds of prime meat and are ready to eat venison, the red meat of monarchs.

Venison is good for you. Deer meat is high in protein and nutrition, and low in fats. It's lower in calories than roast goose, and larger, too. Goose hunters are much heavier eaters and must wear oversized clothes. Venison is heavy in iron, which could put more lead in your pencil.

The preferred foods of our original citizens were the tongue, liver, and heart, and all the fawn meat they could find. A special treat was the buck testicles, thought to pass on mystical powers of the deer: swiftness, surefootedness, and a certain recklessness during the rut.

Is there a noticeable difference between doe and buck meat? Once you cut off the sex stuff, how do you know? An old deer can be tough but if it has been lying around the swamp for a number of years, it could be prime, especially on the side tenderized by its weight. A young animal will not be aged properly unless it's an only child.

 BUCK'S BONUS TIP: **Caution: Eating too much doe meat may dangerously lower testosterone levels in the average male. Which is why the national Democratic Party platform on deer hunting is against trophy hunting. Eating too much buck meat, however, has the reverse effect, often leading to increased domestic discord and higher retail sales in sporting goods emporiums.**

CAUTION: If you haven't been eating much game meat, a sudden diet of it will upset your intestines and you can count on unexpected buildups of gas. These little pockets will slip out at the worst moments, so it's recommended that you eat the first few game meals alone. Once Buck floated a fluffer at dinner that was so terrible it made his older brother lose his dinner through his nose.

CAUTION 2: As one respected old-timer warns, don't pass game gas near an open campfire.

COOKING YOUR DEER: There are many cookbooks on venison cooking, and are either very simple or very complicated. The complicated books are written by constipated unregistered aliens who follow the tradition of Europeans who ruin everything with their fussiness and recipes that run over a page long. You can't expect better from a subcontinent of veneered barbarians that age their meat by hanging the game upside down with guts intact. With their political leanings, they should serve borscht as a side dish. To cook continental style you'd have to own a commercial kitchen and be stuck with shelves full of exotic, equally useless herbs. Forget the food snobs. They never won a world war, and except for the French (who can't but should appreciate the irony), haven't even lost a good Asian conflict. Never trust a recipe over a hundred words, including ingredients.

BUCK'S BONUS TIP: Recent outbreaks of chronic wasting disease worries some health officials but be aware CWD is not the same as the chronic wasting disease hunters contract from working for a large corporation or a large wife. Cautious eaters dress their deer with gloves and discard the brains, however small they may seem. In recent case studies, chronic wasting disease has been shown to be transmitted in the saliva of deer and elk. Which is just another reason NOT to save deer saliva for sauces and marinades.

BONUS RECIPE SECTION

BUCK'S VENISON STEW

Purchase 5 large cans of Dinty Moore® Beef Stew.

Empty all cans into a large pot, heating to a slow boil.

Cook off a pound of your venison stew meat.

Eat the beef out of the stew before your guests arrive.

Add venison and lots of pepper.

BUCK'S JERKY

Leave your scraps out in the sun for a week.

BUCK'S VENISON STEAKS

Cut your steaks an inch thick. Pour two inches of bourbon in your glass. Lightly butter a twelve-inch cast iron frying pan and heat quickly. Slake your thirst with a couple more inches. As soon as the butter browns, lay in the steaks, covered with fresh pepper, and sear. Replace the two inches of bourbon. Quickly remove the steaks. Enjoy! It's not necessary to share the plate or glass.

CANADIAN BAKIN'

Any recipe above can replace the traditional family meal of musk ox, beaver tails, and wild yak milk. Cover the meat with maple syrup, wash down with a warm Molson's, and pop a few maple sugar candy leaves for an after-dinner sweet. Burp.

✔ *SPECIAL NOTE:* Fresh deer innards or guts are choice camp meats. Fresh deer liver is most choice, pan-fried and smothered with caramelized onions. Fresh deer heart, especially fresh fawn heart, comes in a close second only because of its tendency to still beat in the frying pan. Use a tight-fitting lid. Most hunters boil the piss out of the kidneys.

✔ *EXTRA SPECIAL NOTE:* Freezer burn can occur with the best of intentions. Meat fiber crystallizes when not properly wrapped. "Burn" should be cut off and given to the dog humping your leg under the table.

MISCELLANEOUS

POST-SEASON ACTIVITIES

✔ *IN THE WOODS:* Be the last one out of the woods. You may find another person's deer or hunting jacket. In snow country, it's a good time to look for tracks and learn where the deer really were.

If the hunting was poor and you have a few cartridges left, thank the ground squirrels, woodpeckers, and blue jays that made your stand so quiet.

✔ *AT HOME:* You need to catch up on lost sleep. Since you work a full week, snooze during the daylight hours of the weekend. Hunters can take up to nine months to rest from a hard hunt. When awake, your wife and her garden club will want to hear your adventure stories. Often.

✔ *BACK IN THE OFFICE:* Many graduates of Buck's wilderness course like to put certain deer organs in a glass jar to be placed on an office credenza, and hang the trophy head next to the picture of the company founders. By virtue of your superior hunting skills, you have earned the right to wear buckskin, even hair-side out, if your office has casual dress Fridays.

THE WHITE LIES OF DEER HUNTING

We always see deer here!

I've never seen a game warden in this area.

You start dragging—I'll take over when you get tired!

I'll be back with help!

That looks like a legal buck to me!

Try this—it's really good!

No, you don't need a license this far back.

I wouldn't take that kind of crap from him.

Loan me your knife for a while.

No, Honey, this is not a new gun.

Yes, Boss, I'll be back bright and early Monday morning.

They'll never find it here!

I'm doing this because you're my best friend.

That's where I hit it!

It's in my other billfold.

WHAT TO DO WITH THE SPARE PARTS

The holiday season follows on the heels of the hunting season and no finer personal gift can be given to friends and families than mementos of a successful hunt.

✔ *THE HIDE:* Turn it over to a professional tanner and into two gloves, two slippers, or a sleeve for a nice coat. The quality depends on where the bullets went in and how many miles of dead stumps you dragged the animal over. Bullet holes can be made into buttonholes. It's not difficult to do the tanning work yourself, especially if your wife has her own teeth.

✔ *THE FEET:* Cut from the leg and bent before rigor mortis sets in, these can be mounted on a board as a clothes rack gift for your mother-in-law.

✔ *THE ANTLERS:* To be openly displayed to the visiting public. In old times, the antlers were stuck in the barn or garage, but with advances in taxidermy, it's now possible to mount the entire animal for a nature crèche in the family room. Serious hunters add brush, acorn displays, a dead woodpecker, squirrel tails, and fresh scat to complete the deer diorama.

✔ *THE LEGS:* Excellent digging tools for your child's sandbox.

✔ *THE SKULL:* An appropriate desk ornament, the skull cap can keep paper-clips, pushpins, or jellybeans within easy reach.

✔ *THE TEETH:* Donate them to the American Dental Association so they can be polished and whitened and sent to Third World countries like Canada as part of our Peace Corps Dental Assistance Program.

HUNTING INSURANCE

Your regular policy should cover gunshot wounds if accidentally shot in a public conveyance like a bus, plane, or train. Wounds inflicted by beneficiaries are not covered. Heart conditions aggravated by buck fever are covered only if the animal was of trophy dimensions.

✔ *BENEFICIARIES:* Remember your hunting buddies. Don't add to their guilt for accidentally blasting you by not leaving them something so they can make it up to your family, especially your little woman who was last seen getting on a bus with the lawn boy. A permanent tree stand in your backyard would be a fitting memorial.

✔ *EXCEPTION:* Coverage does not include injuries sustained from the accidental discharge of a rifle while your toe is in the trigger guard.

HUNTING ACCIDENTS: Most states have very strict regulations regarding the accidental harvesting of non-resident hunters. Check local regulations.

THE FUTURE OF DEER HUNTING

Some folks ask whether hunting is necessary. On the advice of National Park Service rangers, these armchair anthropologists say that God will reduce the herd to its best level. Aligning with this school of fine thinking are naturalists recommending more natural alternatives of raising more wolves, bobcats, and mountain lions. Clubs of pit bull owners are also lobbying for more freedom in the field.

There is continued interest by the asphalt industry, the used car dealers of America, and the auto repair shop cabal to cut more roads through prime deer habitat. By putting detour signs up at dawn and dusk, these entrepreneurs hope to bring the road hunt up to fifty percent of the total.

Game officials are working hard with the latest technology to learn more about these animals so they can make rational choices in herd size and health. In an attempt to determine "maximum sustainable yield" of herd density, they attach radio collars and insert radio implants for tracking. By turning up the volume of the radios, they can listen in on what deer do in their spare time. Which is not fit to be mentioned in a family-oriented publication like this.

Officials are concerned about the quality of the hunt, not the quantity. Quality time is the new buzzword in hunting. Like divorce counselors, game wardens will ask you if your hunt was as good for you as it was for the carcass draped over your fender.

HUNTER HARASSMENT

Anti-hunters are nipping hard at our heels, trying to take our weapons and animals away from us. The National Rifle Association is trying to keep guns in our holsters but hunters as a group have been subjected to all sorts of written and verbal abuse. We've been caricatured and stereotyped in the non-sporting press and this vilification has inflamed the inadequate loins of the anti-hunter activists.

Fanatics have interrupted trophy game hunts by sending their most suicidal members to step between hunters with large bore rifles and their trophies in remote locations. The organization behind all this has an international reputation for blowing up the wrong boats in foreign harbors and running into Boris' whalers with rubber rafts. They chose rubber believing it's more natural than wood and enjoy the rubber nozzle that inflates the boat, passing it around like an old joint.

The good news is that hunters are finally getting their day in court with hunter non-harassment laws. The laws guarantee a hassle-free hunt and protection from the fuzzy-headed liberals who would hunt if only their women would let them. If a hunter sees a member of an animal rights organization near his camp or smoking in a nonsmoking area, it's possible to make a citizen's arrest for creating a public nuisance. Quietly but firmly arrest the offender and put him or her in your trunk for a roundabout trip to the local constabulary. In a few western states, it's legal to spank the butts of the better-looking female liberals, however rare they may be.

The harassers are easy to identify. They are mostly aging hippies still asking what's called their women if 1968 was their best year, and drive beat-up, original paint Volvo station wagons decorated with "Save the Whales" bumper-stickers. What's called men in that group wear turtlenecks and Earth Shoes, and have granny glasses hanging around their skinny necks. The men would rather be eating a bowl of granola than chasing pipe fitters from Pittsburgh but their larger women and matriarchal mores won't let them. The women would come into the woods but their open-toed Birkenstocks are a liability in a chase up the slopes.

SUNRISE AND SUNSET TIME SCHEDULE

Except in Wisconsin, where resident hunters shoot around the clock, state laws consider a full day of hunting to start 1/2 hour before sunrise until 1/2 hour after sunset. Several states are considering 1/2-day licenses for those who can't stay put in their stand but until these exceptions are made, you're expected to put in a full day. Deer that move between states with differing hours due to variations in daylight saving times are at much higher risk.

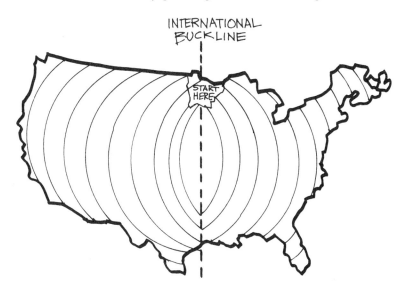

To determine the start of your hunting day, measure from the time guidelines that goes through Buck's stand in northern Minnesota to your stand and add five seconds for each mile west or subtract five seconds for each mile east or vice versa depending on which direction you're facing. In Canada, add one minute either way for each kiloliter of Molson's you drink on the way to the stand. If you are driving deer east of Buck's stand, drivers must shoot first in the early morning, but this is not required in the west. Legal sunrise and sunsets are listed below. Sunrise can be misjudged with car headlights on high or under a full moon and sunsets are tricky sometimes. On a long-distance shot, your deer might be still legal while your shot is questionable. In these borderline cases, stay legal by shooting only in the direction the sun is moving.

INTERNATIONAL BUCKLINE

Sunrise: October 1 to December 31, any year.
Starts at 7:11 A.M. ends at 7:56 A.M.

✔ *NOTE:* Except for late October/early November when the clock is set back an hour for a more leisurely breakfast, add a minute a day or so to determine the legal sunrise.

Sunset: October 1 to December 31, any year.
Starts at 3:54 P.M. ends at 4:34 P.M.

✔ *NOTE:* Allowing for a mid-day snack, subtract a minute or so each day.

EXCUSES

Before you go into the woods, decide if you really want to shoot an animal. If by some genetic mistake, you can't do it, here is a mitt-ful of excuses you can drag out.

IN THE CAMP

Nope. Didn't see nothing. Nope.
Nope. Didn't hear nothing. Nope.
Too cold, warm, wet, dry, windy, snowy.
Won't shoot a flag!
All I saw was does (bucks-only area).

CHAPTER FOUR · MISCELLANEOUS

That stand has never been good.

Was taking a dump.

AT HOME

All I saw was fawns (to children).

Couldn't get a clean shot.

All I saw was does (to wife).

Too cold, warm, wet, dry, windy, snowy.

One more day would have done it but wanted to come home to see my
honey, my kids, mow the lawn, take out the garbage, or clean the garage.

✔ NEVER SAY: "My heart wasn't in it." You'll never get out of the house again.

THE BIG SECRET

DON'T LET YOUR WIFE READ THIS PART!

If your hunting expeditions are still being sold as bringing home the bacon,
you now only have to walk as far as your corner telephone booth. Yes, what
you've scaled mountains, humped hedgerows, and sat in cold, creaky deer
stands for is now available through mail order. Thanks to modern animal
husbandry and a expanding interest for game meat in fine restaurants, your
furred friends can be ordered like you order pizza, by telephone.

Originally designed as a convenience to institutional food buyers, the
new consumer service can be habit-forming for those who chill too quickly,
whose joints ache after a day pounding cornfields, and whose eyes no longer
coordinate with the trigger finger. Of course, the terrible temptation would
be to pack up as usual, kiss the loved ones goodbye, drive directly to the local
flashing "Beer Here" sign to call in your orders, and hole up with your cronies
for a busman's holiday. But think how nice it would be to walk in on Sunday
night and tell the little woman wearing the lawn boy's tee shirt the hunt was

great, and Bambi's dad is being processed and can be picked up next week. The little woman will think you are a saint. Your choice of off-site processing will soften your daughter's opinion of your barbaric blood sports. Your hunting prowess will be telegraphed around the cul-de-sac, forcing your yuppie neighbors to button up about the snowmobile collection in different stages of disrepair in your driveway. You will be dubbed "Old Sureshot" and your property values will increase.

Have your friendly butcher call the order in so the meat can be delivered direct. Order the choicest cuts—leg, loin, oysters—so your loved ones won't have to eat camp meats that diminish your parental authority.

Orders can take a week so schedule your call accordingly. Order only slightly more than last season's game bag. Nobody likes a game hog. These farmed deer may be small by Buck's standards but most likely so are you. Be smart: don't order three back legs. Even your spawn raised on the Disney channel know that most deer don't have that many back legs. Take more, not fewer dollars from the joint savings account (inflation being what it is), and salt away any savings. After a couple of seasons, you'll have enough set aside to take a real safari to an even more exotic, target-rich location. Remember: what happens in Vegas, stays in Vegas.

AFTERWORD

WHY NOT HUNT DEER?

Only the really stupid deer are shot. As a deer hunter, you are part of natural selection, just what Darwin and his Southern Baptist followers have said all along. Deer hunting accidents are God's way of culling dummies out of our ranks.

Now that you've had a chance to absorb centuries' worth of advice, it's up to you to make it happen. Buck knows it's easier to stay home feigning illness, death in the families, job pressures, and all kinds of deadlines. Sometimes it's cold and nasty out there. Sometimes it isn't fun at all. But it's only once a year, and only a hunter can properly pass down new traditions and old clothes.

Did Buck forget anything? Let me know. But for now, Buck stops here.

Buck Peterson and some of his woodland friends after an afternoon romp in northernmost Minnesota. The cabin is an outbuilding on his preserve, within rifle shot of the lodge and home of Buck and his hunting pig, Dorothy. Buck has hunted deer in all 50 states, one radioactive atoll, three national parks, all Canadian provinces, the lost Kingdom of Islandia, and, dressed as Goofy, after hours in the Magic Kingdom. His first deer rifle was a Springfield 03-A3, 30-06 with open sights. Buck can be found reloading at www.buckpeterson.com.